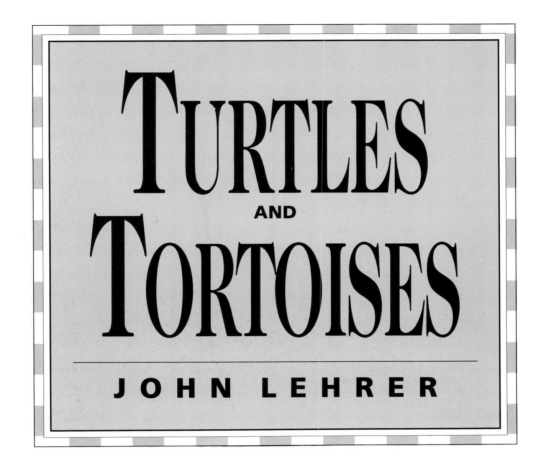

TURTLES
AND
TORTOISES

JOHN LEHRER

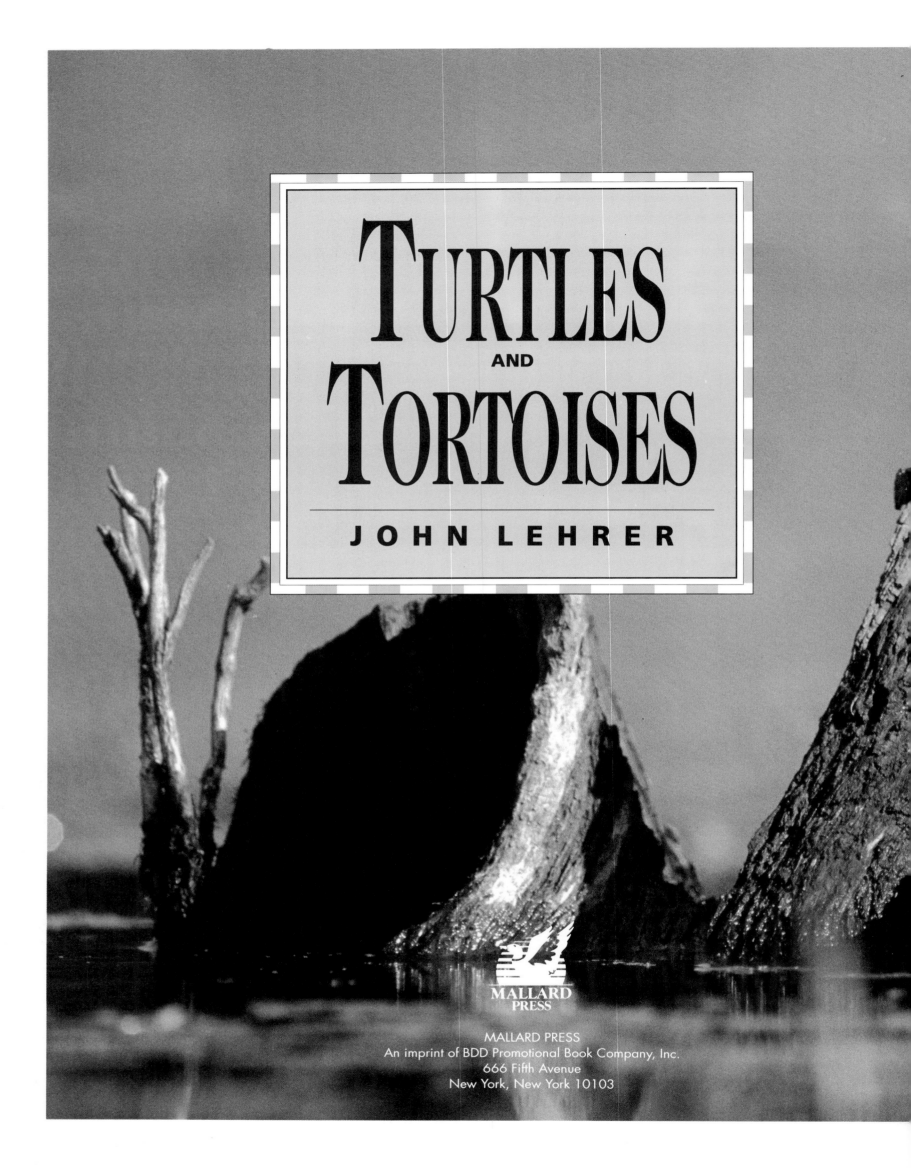

TURTLES
AND
TORTOISES

JOHN LEHRER

MALLARD
PRESS

MALLARD PRESS
An imprint of BDD Promotional Book Company, Inc.
666 Fifth Avenue
New York, New York 10103

A FRIEDMAN GROUP BOOK

Published by MALLARD PRESS
An imprint of BDD Promotional Book
Company, Inc.
666 Fifth Avenue
New York, New York 10103

Mallard Press and its accompanying design and
logo are trademarks of BDD Promotional
Book Company, Inc.

ISBN 0-792-45290-9

TURTLES AND TORTOISES
was prepared and produced by
Michael Friedman Publishing Group, Inc.
15 West 26th Street
New York, New York 10010

Editor: Sharon Kalman
Art Director: Jeff Batzli
Designer: Kingsley Parker
Photography Editor: Christopher Bain
Production: Karen L. Greenberg

Typeset by BPE Graphics
Color separation by Universal Colour Scanning Ltd.
Printed and bound in Hong Kong by Leefung-Asco
Printers, Ltd.

CONTENTS

INTRODUCTION

For as long as I can remember I have been fascinated by reptiles. Like millions of other American children, I was given a baby turtle as one of my first pets—a red-eared slider, which we mistakenly called a "painted" turtle—when I was quite young. Through ignorance, I fed it fish food and kept it in a small tank with too much water and too little dry land. In a short time it died, as do most pet turtles.

When I was eight or nine I spent many summer days in my hometown of Sandusky, Ohio, roaming the banks of Pipe Creek, near a cemetery on the outskirts of town. Mostly I looked for garter snakes, which I'd take home (much to my mother's dismay) and keep in a glass-sided terrarium my father built. Occasionally, I came across adult painted turtles. I took them home, too, but later released them because I did not have an adequate place to keep them.

I read a lot as a child, and some of my relatives inadvertently encouraged my interest in reptiles: My grandmother gave me Raymond L. Ditmars' classic work, *Snakes of the World,* and a great aunt gave me Holling Clancy Holling's *Minn of the Mississippi,* which I still consider a superb book on snapping turtles.

Shortly thereafter I stopped collecting snakes and turtles, turning to more conventional pets such as cats and dogs, but I've never lost my interest or affection for this ancient class of animal. Whenever I visit a natural history museum, zoo, or pet shop, I invariably head for the reptiles first.

Though turtles, like snakes, are reptiles, somehow they have always seemed different to me and, apparently, to many others. Turtle expert Archie Carr summarized the feelings of millions when he said: "Most people have a vague feeling that no reptiles except turtles are to be trusted." I have always thought that of all the reptiles, turtles seem the most approachable and innocuous. Snakes and crocodilians, by comparison, seem slightly sinister, although no less interesting for it. As for lizards, they have always seemed to me to be misfits, an attempt at a snake that didn't quite succeed.

Yes, turtles definitely are appealing creatures. People readily develop the same sort of warm feelings for turtles otherwise reserved for hamsters, rabbits, guinea pigs, and kittens—except, of course, those people who regard turtles primarily as a source of food.

Apart from the feelings of affinity and affection they evoke, turtles are interesting because they are not quite what they seem. On land, they may be awkward and slow, but in water, the natural element for many, they are creatures of speed and grace. Similarly, the turtle's shell creates the sense that it is a simple, one-dimensional, somewhat comical creature, and throughout history the turtle has been the butt of many fables and jokes. In fact, the turtle's shell is a remarkable feat of natural engineering that, in its differing forms, has assisted the turtle in adapting to a variety of environments.

In this book I want to enlarge the reader's awareness of the complexity of this tough, adaptable animal, which has thrived on Earth for more than 150 million years. To this end, I have described in nontechnical terms the turtle's body structure and how it works, given a fairly complete overview of the various turtle families, and provided interesting details of the life patterns of many individual species. In the final chapter, I describe the complex and frequently disastrous relationships between turtles and human beings.

I have not attempted to write an exhaustive or scientific description of all facets of turtle anatomy, physiology, and behavior. Instead, I have presented the most appealing turtles here, to provide the most comprehensive overview possible. A number of books, many of which are listed in the bibliography (page 124), describe most of the known facts about the more than two hundred species of turtles.

A few words about terminology. "Turtle," "tortoise," and "terrapin" are terms commonly used to describe the subject of this book, and usage varies according to culture. For instance, the British generally use the term "turtle" to refer only to sea turtles; other shelled reptiles are referred to as tortoises.

In America, all species that are semiaquatic or fully aquatic are called turtles (for instance, painted turtles and leatherback turtles); the term "tortoise" refers to species that live primarily on land (the desert tortoise, for example). The term "terrapin," derived from a Native American word, is used primarily to mean any turtle that is sold to be eaten (referring mostly to the diamondback terrapin, but also to cooters and sliders).

Strictly speaking, however, the term "turtle" is correct when applied to any shelled reptile.

TURTLE BIOLOGY

What a remarkable animal is the turtle! Consider: Prototurtles evolved more than 200 million years ago, and giant ancestors of turtles shared the earth with dinosaurs during the Golden Age of Reptiles. The turtle survived the demise of the dinosaurs, and in its present form has thrived for upwards of 150 million years. That's three times as long as modern mammals and more than 3,000 times as long as *Homo sapiens* have inhabited the planet.

A turtle may be defined as a reptile with a bony or leathery shell into which its head and limbs can be partly or, in some cases, fully retracted. Turtles have no teeth; instead, they have beaklike jaws with a sharp cutting edge. Turtles have four strong legs, usually equipped with claws, suitable for walking, crawling, or swimming, plus a tail.

At first glance, human beings find turtles attractive because their shells are so prominent. For most people, a turtle is its shell; the terms become synonymous. This is both ironic and unfortunate—ironic because while in a literal sense the shell does provide protection for the turtle's internal and external body parts, it also creates a barrier, hiding the complex physiological reality of the turtle from those who find turtles interesting but inaccessible.

The shell's prominence also creates the sense that turtles are simpler and less diverse animals than they actually are. In fact, there are a dozen distinctly different major types, or families, of turtles and more than 200 species in all.

Turtles live in most of the temperate, semitropical, and tropical regions of the globe in almost any imaginable surroundings—woods, ponds, rivers, lakes, marshlands, prairies, deserts, and the open ocean. In the wild, most turtles are omnivorous, eating food as varied as insects, tender seagrasses, carrion, fruit, and fish. A few, however, are either carnivorous or vegetarians.

Turtles range in size from a few inches in length (the eastern mud turtle, for example, found in the eastern United States) to the largest of all turtles, a sea turtle known as the leatherback, which inhabits tropical waters and may reach nearly 8 feet (3 meters) in length and weigh as much as 1,500 pounds (560 kilograms).

If any qualities can be said to characterize turtles, then, it is their ability to adapt and to endure. Having developed a body type that suits its needs for obtaining food as well as for protecting and reproducing itself, the turtle's continued well-being on the planet is threatened only by the inconsiderate and/or wantonly destructive actions of humans.

SCIENTIFIC CLASSIFICATION AND REPTILE EVOLUTION

In order to understand how animals and plants are both similar to and different from one another, scientists categorize them according to a classification system devised by the Swedish botanist Carolus Linnaeus in the 1700s.

Linnaeus' system, consisting of nine levels (shown below), is hierarchical, meaning that the categories at the top of the list ("kingdom," "phylum") refer to the broadest and most significant distinctions among groups of plants and animals, and those categories at the bottom ("genus," "species") refer to less significant distinctions that, nevertheless, mark one animal and plant as identical to or different from another. Thus, the animal kingdom includes all animals, but the family of turtles known as Chelydridae includes only snapping turtles.

CLASSIFICATION OF THE ALLIGATOR SNAPPING TURTLE

What follows is the scientific way to categorize the largest freshwater turtle in the United States, the alligator snapper, which is found in the rivers, canals, lakes, swamps, and ponds of southern and south-central states:

Kingdom:	Animalia	All animals
Phylum:	Chordata	Animals with a notochord
Subphylum:	Vertebrata	Vertebrates (animals with backbones)
Class:	Reptilia	All reptiles
Order:	Chelonia*	All turtles (and tortoises)
Suborder:	Cryptodira	Straight-necked turtles
Family:	Chelydridae	Snapping turtles
Genus:	*Macroclemys*	Distinguished by three prominent ridges on the carapace (upper shell), extra scutes, and lateral eye placement
Species:	*temmincki*	Alligator snapping turtle

*Depending on the source consulted, the order name for turtles is either "Chelonia," "Testudinata," or "Testudines."

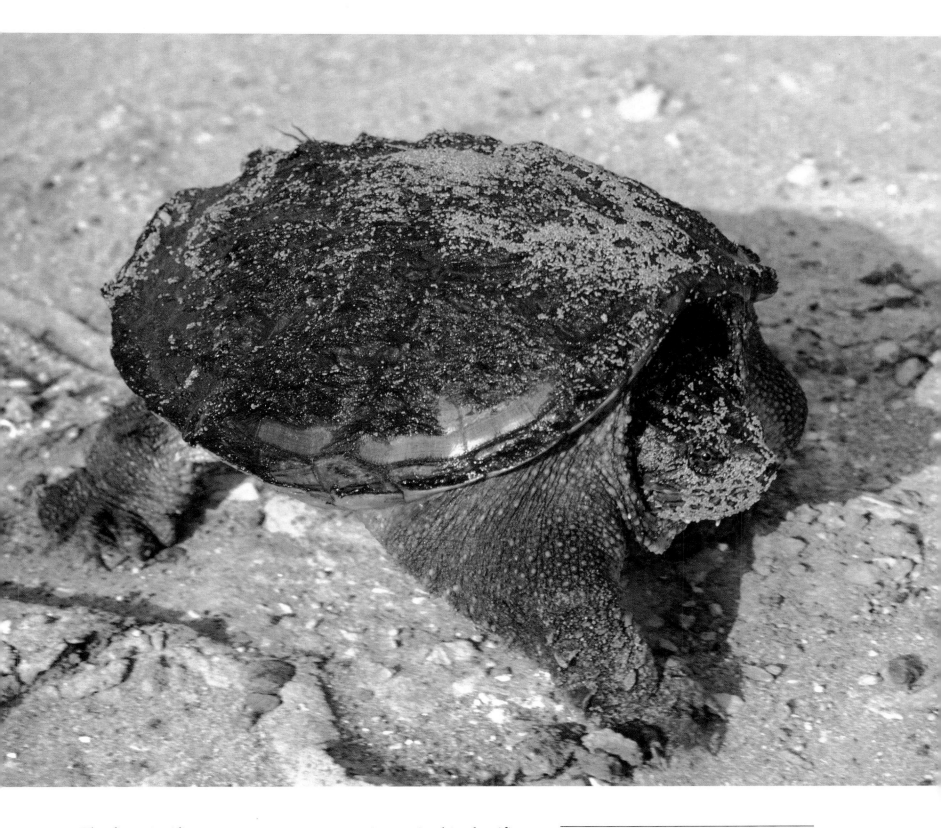

A common snapping turtle casts a wary eye upon an intruder into its domain.

The first significant category to pay attention to in this classification scheme is subphylum: Animals either have backbones (vertebrates) or they don't (invertebrates).

Turtles belong to the group of animals known as reptiles (Reptilia), one of five classes of animals in the world that are vertebrates. Reptiles are considered a more advanced form of vertebrate than are amphibians (Amphibia) and fish (Pisces), but less advanced than birds (Aves) and mammals (Mammalia).

As suggested earlier, contemporary reptiles are the survivors of a much more extensive group of animals that evolved from amphibians and flourished during the Mesozoic era, which lasted from about 230 million years ago until 70 million years ago.

Reptiles were the dominant form of life at this time. They ranged in size from those as small as present-day lizards to perhaps the largest animal ever to inhabit the earth, the recently discovered *Seismosaurus,* which may have reached a length of 120 feet (44 meters) and a weight of 90 tons (82 metric tons). Reptiles of this time adapted to every kind of environment—swamps, deserts, forests, grasslands, rivers, lakes, oceans, even the air.

Toward the end of the Mesozoic era, fossil evidence indicates that the dinosaurs and about 80 percent of the other living reptiles died out rather suddenly (geologically speaking) for reasons still not clearly understood. Their dominant position was taken by the higher vertebrates, birds, and mammals.

Today, reptiles still make up an important part of the animal kingdom; almost 6,000 species, mostly lizards and snakes, still exist. They help preserve the delicate balance of nature by eliminating large numbers of rodents, insects, and other pests.

Returning to the classification system, turtles are an order (one of four) within the class of reptiles; the three other living orders are snakes and lizards (Squamata); crocodiles, caimans, and alligators (Crocodilia); and the tuatara (Rhynchocephalia), a rare, lizardlike reptile that lives only on a few islands near New Zealand.

What makes reptiles different from other vertebrate classes are the following qualities, which are shared by turtles: a skin covered with scales or horny plates; a pair of lungs to breathe air; a body temperature that fluctuates with the environment; reproduction by internal fertilization; the ability to lay tough, durable eggs on land; and offspring that look and act like miniature adults.

A passing familiarity with scientific classification is all the lay person interested in turtles requires. For the purposes of this book, then, I'll make an important distinction between suborders in the section on turtle anatomy that follows and then primarily discuss different families and species of turtles, mostly using the common name rather than the Latin name for the animal.

The Florida box turtle's hinged plastron enables it to completely close itself off from the world outside.

© A.B. Sheldon

Modern turtles evolved from small animals known as cotylosaurs, or "stem" reptiles, which lived about 250 million years ago and from which all reptile lines have evolved. The first true turtles—equipped with bony or leathery shells and with a scissorlike jaw in place of teeth—appeared during the Triassic period, a little more than 200 million years ago.

During the Mesozoic era, turtles were a far more varied order than they are today. In fact, turtles were divided into three suborders, one of which is now extinct. They evolved in ways that suited their habitats, developing light, leathery shells and large, powerful legs with webbed feet for swimming, or high, domed, bony shells and elephant-like legs for living on land.

Fossil remains of early turtles have been found in Europe, North America, South America, Asia, Africa, and Australia. Many were the size of modern turtles, but some were much larger than any turtles presently living. A fossil of a tortoise shell measuring 6 feet (2 meters) in length, for instance, was found in India, and remains of sea turtles reaching nearly 11 feet (4 meters) in length were found in the United States.

Any discussion of turtle anatomy has to begin with that most obvious element of turtle architecture, the shell. Most vertebrates have an internal skeleton that is covered with muscle tissue (flesh) protected by scales, hair, feathers, or, in the case of humans, skin. Turtles are the opposite, having their skeletons on the outside of their bodies which protects the flesh and vital organs contained within. Some people have the notion that a turtle's body is contained inside the shell, and that somehow it might be possible (and easier) for the turtle to get around if only it could unburden itself of its shell. But that's not true: The shell is part and parcel of the turtle's body.

A turtle's shell has two parts: a convex dorsal (upper) section called the carapace, and a flat, belly section called the plastron. These two units are connected by bony bridges on the sides of the shell, which leave gaps at the front and back for the turtle's head, tail, and four legs to protrude.

Both the carapace and the plastron are composed of two layers. The inner layer of each consists of a mosaic of tightly joined bones. The turtle's spine is rigid, immobile, in fact, because the turtle's vertebrae and ribs have become an integral part of the inner layer of the carapace. Only the legs, neck, and tail can move.

The outer layer of the shell is made up of a symmetrical pattern of broad, horny scales (scutes). The seams of the inner and outer layers of the carapace and plastron don't coincide, which makes the integrity of the total shell much stronger.

Some species of turtles have a plastron that is hinged in one or more places. This feature allows it to flex and completely enclose the turtle's head, tail, and legs.

Turtle shells are complex and vary in their makeup from family to family; what follows is a general description of the outer layer of the carapace typical of tortoises and pond and marsh turtles, which constitute more than half the living species (see diagram).

ANCESTRAL TURTLES

CHELONIAN ANATOMY

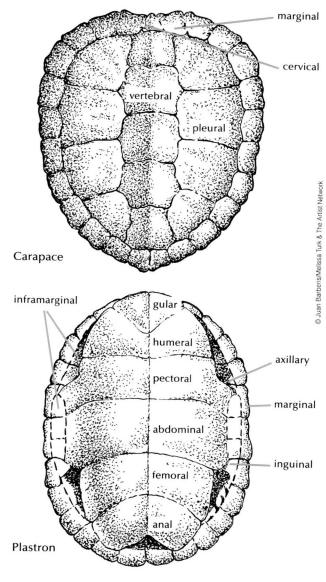

SCUTES OF THE TURTLE SHELL.

© A.B. Sheldon

Above: The symmetrically decorated plastron of a yellow-bellied turtle, a medium-sized North American emydid. *Right:* This Florida soft-shelled turtle is able to lie on the bottom of a river in shallow water and stretch its neck to the surface to breathe.

© Dr. E.R. Degginger

Usually, there is a series of five large scutes running from front to back along the midline of the carapace; these are known as the vertebrals or centrals. On either side is a row of four larger scutes, known as costals or laterals. Around the edge are a series of about twenty-four smaller scutes, called marginals. Just above the head is a small scute known as the nuchal, and just above the tail is a scute termed the supracaudal.

Many modern turtles no longer require the heavy armor-plated shells their ancestors needed for protection from dinosaurs and other large reptiles. So, in the course of evolution, the shape and composition of the turtle's shell have adapted to the environment inhabited by a particular type of turtle.

For instance, it would be very difficult for a turtle to swim with a bony, heavy, high-arched shell such as tortoises possess. Sea turtles, therefore, have developed relatively sleek shells (plus broad flippers that move in breast-stroke fashion), which allow them to move rapidly through the water at speeds (for short distances) comparable to the fastest human runners.

The soft-shell turtle, such as those found in North America, has developed a shell with a flat, rounded shape that is also covered by a tough, leathery skin. This allows it to burrow easily in the soft bottoms of streams and ponds, camouflaging its body until a tasty meal appears.

Apart from its shell, the turtle's neck is probably the most interesting and significant part of its anatomy. Long and very mobile, a turtle's neck is made up of eight vertebral segments (mammals have seven).

In fact, it's the flexible nature of the neck (and the surrounding muscles and skin) that allows a turtle to pull its head back into its shell. Turtles withdraw their heads in two different ways, and this determines one of the primary methods of classifying them.

Side-necked turtles (suborder Pluerodira) withdraw their heads by pulling their necks to the side. At one time, species of Pleurodira lived in North America, Europe, Asia, South America, Africa, and Australia, but for unknown reasons became extinct. Now, side-necked turtles live only in South America, Africa, and Australia.

The dominant form of turtles in the world today belong to the suborder Cryptodira, sometimes called "straight-necked" or "hidden-necked" turtles. Turtles of this suborder pull their necks straight back into their shells. Viewed from the side, their necks take on the shape of an S-curve when withdrawn.

Several other features of the turtle's anatomy are distinctive and deserve mention. The first is the turtle's skull, which is unlike that of other reptiles and is considered primitive (meaning that it has changed very little from that of fossil turtles). Termed "anapsid," it has a solid cranium and no openings near the temples.

As has been mentioned, contemporary turtles have no teeth, though rudimentary dentition has been found in some fossil skulls. Jaw shapes vary from species to species, but most function like the blades of scissors, shearing animal flesh and plants with their sharp, horned edges.

THE NECK AND OTHER PARTS

An easy way to lose a finger: The imposing jaws of a common snapping turtle.

A Florida gopher tortoise, which digs long burrows often shared by other creatures.

A turtle's skin is tough and scaly but flexible, especially at the neck, where wrinkles and folds allow for extension and withdrawal of the head. The legs are often covered with somewhat larger, thicker, overlapping scales for greater protection. The nails on the feet of many turtles are quite sharp and are useful for digging and climbing.

Finally, an unusual feature of chelonian anatomy is that because of the all-encompassing nature of the turtle's shell, the pectoral and pelvic limb girdles (to which the turtle's legs are attached) are within the rib cage. In most animals, they are above and below, respectively.

TURTLE PHYSIOLOGY

If turtle anatomy is unorthodox and fascinating, turtle physiology—the way their bodies work—is even more so.

Take, for instance, the way turtles breathe. Mammals, birds, and even other reptiles can take air into their lungs by expanding the chest cavity, but because their ribs are part of the carapace and their shells are rigid, turtles must use another method.

Turtles inhale by means of two muscles located next to the hind leg sockets, below the vital organs. When these expand, they allow air to enter the lungs, much the same way the diaphragm works in mammals. To exhale, turtles use a third, complex muscle that pushes the vital organs against the lungs, forcing the air out.

Alternative methods of breathing are necessary, however, because when a turtle senses danger and withdraws its head and legs into its shell, the air in its lungs is forced out (sometimes producing a hissing sound, which many people mistakenly interpret as a hostile gesture). If a turtle is threatened for a long period of time, it may have to survive with its lungs almost emptied of air. And what about aquatic turtles, which spend long periods of time submerged?

As it turns out, turtles do have other, less obvious ways of taking in oxygen: Some aquatic turtles are able to use their mouths as a kind of gill, drawing water in through their nasal openings, isolating and absorbing the oxygen, then expelling the water. Soft-shelled turtles are also able to absorb oxygen through their skin, and some aquatic turtles can absorb oxygen through thin-walled sacs located near their anal openings.

It may seem that these alternative breathing methods wouldn't take in much oxygen, which might be true. But turtles don't require as much oxygen as many other animals do. This has less to do with their activity levels (to think that all turtles are lethargic and slow-moving is a mistake) than with the way their bodies operate.

When most animals, including man, hold their breath for a period of time, they have to begin breathing again not so much because they lack oxygen as because they can't tolerate the buildup of carbon dioxide in their lungs. Turtles, however, are able to tolerate high levels of carbon dioxide, improving their ability to survive without breathing. Furthermore, when aquatic turtles dive, their heartbeat slows down, lowering the demand for oxygen.

This gives some turtles the ability, for example, to go for several days underwater without breathing in their normal way. In fact, the late Archie Carr, a herpetologist who spent much of his life studying

Below: Different jaw types among turtles (*left to right*): the parrotlike beak of the big-headed turtle (*Platysternon megacephalum*) of Southeast Asia; fleshy lips cover the sharp, horny jaws of a soft-shell (*Trionyx* species); the alligator snapper (*Macroclemys temminicki*) has a hooked beak for taking prey; similar to the alligator snapper, the leatherback's (*Dermochelys coriacea*) jaw also has a hooked beak for catching prey; the short, broad beak of the giant Aldabra tortoise (*Megalochelys gigantea*) is ideally shaped for chewing vegetation; the Indian roofed turtle has serrated jaws for eating water plants.

and working to preserve the sea turtle, described an instance in which a turtle survived for twenty-four hours in a container filled completely with nitrogen.

"COLD-BLOODEDNESS"

A few words should be said about turtle metabolism. Reptiles, turtles included, are often termed "cold-blooded" to contrast them with birds and mammals. However, this term is misleading.

Birds and mammals—man, for instance—are known as "endotherms," meaning that they maintain a constant body temperature, which is regulated by internal mechanisms.

Turtles and other reptiles (also fish and amphibians) are termed "ectotherms," meaning that their body temperature is much more dependent on the temperature of the surrounding environment. Ectotherms practice "behavioral temperature control," which means that they control their body temperature by seeking out or avoiding warm ground or sunlight.

Turtles take in much of the heat they need from basking in the sun; this is true for all types of turtles and tortoises, aquatic as well as those who live on land. Different species require different ranges of temperatures to thrive.

A concern with ambient temperature is less important for turtles living in tropical regions (especially forests, where variations of temperature and humidity are minimal), but it is another matter for turtles living in temperate regions. When the temperature begins to drop in early fall, many turtles prepare for several months of hibernation. This holds true even for turtles and tortoises kept as pets in places such as southern California, where the overnight temperature in midwinter rarely drops below 40°F (4°C) and the temperature at midday may be more than 70°F (21°C).

TURTLE PHYSIOLOGY

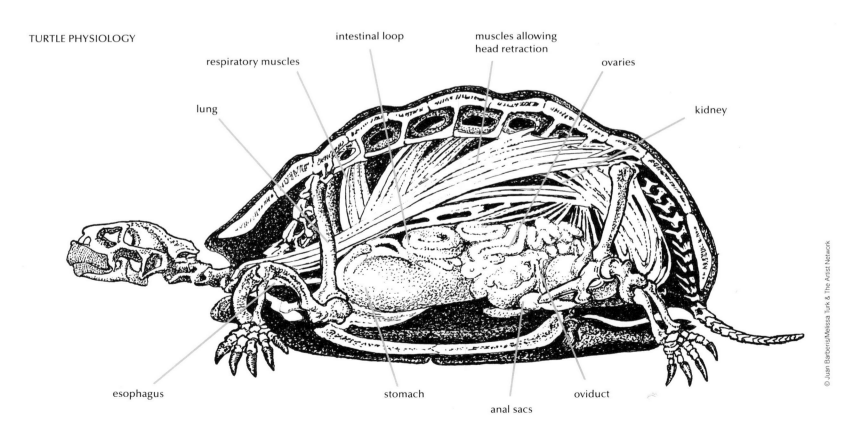

respiratory muscles

intestinal loop

muscles allowing head retraction

ovaries

lung

kidney

esophagus

stomach

anal sacs

oviduct

Among aquatic turtles, the variety that makes its way into the northernmost waters is the leatherback; although it nests exclusively in tropical and semitropical regions, individuals have been spotted as far north as the coast of the maritime provinces of Canada.

Humans often think that because of the burden of their shells, turtles are clumsy and lead sedentary, slow-paced lives. Such a conclusion is inaccurate. Certainly the shell, which may account for one-third of a turtle's weight, must be accommodated, but most turtles are agile, strong walkers or swimmers. What they lack in speed, they make up for in endurance and persistence.

TURTLE LOCOMOTION

A turtle's legs and feet are shaped for its environment and style of locomotion (*top to bottom*): Pond turtles have scaled feet with well-developed claws on the front and only moderately webbed rear feet; river turtles' feet are more webbed, enabling them both to swim well and to move about on land; the front legs of sea turtles take the form of flippers and move in a breast-stroke fashion; soft-shell turtles have webbed feet with only three claws; tortoises use their flattened forelimbs to dig, while their elephantine hind legs provide sturdy support on land.

© Manny Rubio

In spite of the burden of its shell, many turtles are good climbers. Here, an African pancake tortoise descends some rocks.

How a turtle gets around depends, of course, on its habitat, and over the millions of years turtles have lived on Earth, different species have adapted well to the parts of the globe they inhabit. Different families of turtles have developed almost a half-dozen distinct varieties of limbs to assist in their movement.

The giant tortoises of the Galapagos Islands, for instance, travel from the coast to high, mountain plateaus, raising their heavy bodies off the ground as they walk. So strong are their legs and shells that they could carry the weight of a human on their backs and still continue to move along. Sea turtles, whose forelimbs have evolved into paddles or flippers, are excellent swimmers, moving through the water rapidly and gracefully. Amphibious turtles, who divide their time between land and ponds, rivers, or lakes, often have webbed feet that serve them well for walking or swimming.

Turtles use a number of different senses to carry out the primary activities of their lives: finding food, avoiding danger, and courtship and mating.

The senses of sight and smell are most important to turtles, because both are used to obtain food. The eyesight of most turtles, for instance, is quite sharp, particularly at short distances. Their long-distance vision and ability to notice different forms is good, too, even under water. Experiments have determined that turtles also can discriminate between lines of different widths and can distinguish a variety of colors: red, yellow, green, blue, and violet. They make finer distinctions among colors at the red end of the spectrum. Turtles can also distinguish different types of food by sight.

Turtles' eyes are protected by their eyelids; their eyes also have large tear ducts. This latter feature is especially noticeable in sea turtles, who "weep" when laying their eggs. This occurrence has given rise to folktales that the animals are in pain or feel sad about leaving the eggs. In fact, the tears serve to wash sand from the turtle's eyes. It is interesting to note that turtles shed tears at the same rate underwater.

Even more important than keen eyesight to the task of searching for food, however, is a turtle's sense of smell. Accomplished by means of the nostrils and (as with other reptiles) the Jacobson's organ, the sense of smell is perhaps the turtle's most efficient and powerful method of perception. The sections of the turtle's brain having to do with smell are large and well developed.

Aquatic turtles can even find food in cloudy water with their sense of smell. Also, both sea turtles and land tortoises search out and recognize potential mates, as well as other turtles of the same species, by sniffing, particularly in the anal region, where glands secrete odorous substances specific to a turtle's sex and species. Female turtles also may find their nesting grounds partly by their senses of taste and smell. Some authorities think that when a female baby sea turtle hatches on a beach, it tastes the sand, and this makes an imprint in its memory. Years later, based on that recollection, the adult sea turtle makes its way back to the same beach. (Turtles apparently have a well-developed sense of taste: They will sometimes reject food after taking a bite, perhaps indicating that they object to the way it tastes.)

It would seem that turtles can't hear well at all; at least, they're not able to easily or proficiently distinguish types of sounds from one another. Turtles have well-developed ears, although it's often difficult to determine the external location because it's frequently covered by one or more scales.

Turtles do, however, have what some sources term a "seismic" sense: They can detect low-frequency vibrations transmitted from the ground. They seem to have an accurate sense of the distance of the source of the vibration and whether it represents a danger to their well-being.

It's not clear whether turtles have voices, though some species definitely are able to make distinctive noises by exhaling, grinding, or clicking their jaws. Most vocal noises made by turtles occur during mating. The giant male Galapagos tortoises roar at five-second

SENSES, PERCEPTION, AND INTELLIGENCE

© A.B. Sheldon

Two North American emydids: (*above*) a juvenile false map turtle, which lives in the central United States; (*below*) the abundant river cooter, which is found throughout the southern United States.

© Dr. E.R. Degginger

© Gerry Ellis/Ellis Wildlife Collection

© Gerry Ellis/Ellis Wildlife Collection

Above: A giant tortoise from Indefatigable Island in the Galapagos. These tortoises were heavily exploited for their oil until at least the 1930s, perhaps even later. *Left:* A red-eared slider, the most common pet turtle in the world.

intervals. The big-headed turtle of Southeast Asia is reputed to squeak or scream when picked up. It's probably accurate to say, however, that turtles don't communicate with each other in any significant way by means of uttered sounds.

Many turtles also display a discriminating sense of touch. For instance, a part of the courting behavior of some male painted turtles is to gently stroke the face of the female with their long claws as they swim near the females. Also, female turtles, when laying eggs, can dig a hole of the correct size and shape, as well as arrange and bury their eggs without looking at what they're doing—completely by a sense of touch.

Most humans find that clean, healthy turtles give off no odor, except for certain varieties of musk and mud turtles—known popularly as stinkpots and stinkjims—that give off a foul, musky odor as a means of self-protection, much as a skunk does. If these animals are kept as pets, they will stop giving off the odor once they've become acclimated to humans.

Are turtles intelligent? In some ways, asking such a question is pointless because it's too general and anthropocentric. What is meant by the term "intelligent," after all? Turtles are capable of amazing feats, especially where navigation and sense of direction are concerned. And something must be said for the animal's ability to adapt and survive for so many millions of years. But these qualities, admirable as they are, may have more to do with something like instinct rather than intelligence.

Turtle intelligence is not a subject that has been much studied. Experiments have shown that a turtle can learn fairly readily to slowly work its way through an elementary maze, but turtles certainly lack the sort of problem-solving abilities characteristic of mice. Similarly, it's undoubtedly futile to attempt to teach a turtle the sorts of tricks a dog might take to readily, such as "fetch," "roll over," or "play dead."

On the other hand, turtles kept in captivity respond to, and in some cases seem to recognize their owners, particularly persons responsible for feeding them. Anecdotes have been recorded of pet turtles who wait by the refrigerator at feeding time and turtles in zoos that learn when feeding time is.

In *The Running Press Book of Turtles,* author Richard Nicholls, quoting naturalist Henry Beston's *The Outermost House,* offers perhaps the most pertinent remarks about turtle intelligence:

> For the animal shall not be measured by man. In a world older and more complete than ours they move finished and complete, gifted with extensions of the senses we have lost or never attained, living by voices we shall never hear. They are not brethren, they are not underlings; they are other nations, caught with ourselves in the net of life and time, fellow prisoners of the splendour and travail of the earth.

COURTSHIP, MATING, AND REPRODUCTION

SEXUAL MATURITY AND SEXUAL DIFFERENTIATION

Among turtles, courtship, mating, and reproduction are complex and mysterious phenomena—less so, fortunately, for the turtles involved in the process than for humans attempting to understand it.

The first factor complicating the understanding of turtle sexuality is that not only do different species of turtles reach sexual maturity at different ages, the same is sometimes true for turtles of the same species.

For instance, male stinkpots, a variety of freshwater musk turtle found in North America, become sexually mature at age three or four, but females do not reach sexual maturity until their ninth to eleventh year, according to one study. (Another puts the ages at three years and two to seven years, respectively.) Male and female gopher tortoises, on the other hand, reach sexual maturity in fifteen to twenty years.

Second, because the sexual organs are internal (within the cloaca), it's sometimes difficult for a human to tell a male turtle from a female, especially if there are no distinctive secondary sexual characteristics for that species.

Especially difficult varieties to differentiate sexually include certain species of snapping turtles and tortoises. (Again, this is a problem only for humans. Turtles themselves have no difficulty in this regard.)

In general, the following external characteristics can be used to distinguish male turtles from females, though not all occur together in a single species:

Mating Galapagos tortoises. Different species of turtles have their own distinctive courtship and mating rituals.

The plastron of the female is flat, whereas that of the male may be slightly concave. This makes it easier for him to mount the female's carapace, and remain mounted during intercourse. Usually, the carapace of the female is more steeply curved and higher than that of the male.

The tail of the male is longer and thicker than that of the female. Also, the distance from the cloaca to the back edge of the plastron is greater in the male. Some male turtles have a strong horn on the tips of their tails that curves under the female's carapace during intercourse.

On many amphibious turtles, such as the red-eared slider, the front claws of the male are much longer.

It's difficult to generalize about the overall size of male versus female turtles, so this is neither an easy nor foolproof way to tell the sexes apart. In many species, the adult male and female are of about equal size. In the case of the alligator snapping turtle and some giant tortoises, the males are much bigger. In many species of painted turtles, however, the female may grow to be more than twice as large as the male. Male diamondback terrapins are also generally much smaller than females. The same is true of color. In other animals—birds, for instance—the male is generally the more brightly colored of the sexes. With turtles, males sometimes have more distinctive coloring, but the differences are generally far less marked.

COURTSHIP BEHAVIOR AND MATING

Courtship and mating for most varieties of turtles begins in the spring. Sperm has been produced in the testes of the male the previous year and stored in the epididymis over the winter. In temperate climates, where turtles are active from April through October, male turtles come out of hibernation ready to mate. In the tropics, where turtles are active year round, mating begins with the rainy season.

Female turtles, too, begin producing eggs late in the year, and ovulation starts in May or June of the following year. At this time, the eggs are 70 to 90 percent of their full size.

During mating season, female turtles usually remain in their normal habitats, and males seek them out. Some land-dwelling species may travel several miles in search of a partner; sea turtles travel much farther.

At first, a male recognizes a female of the same species by sight, but then he checks her out by sniffing her anal region, where the odorous substances she emits let him know whether he has made the right choice. This procedure is the same for aquatic turtles.

Courtship always precedes mating, and courtship rituals among turtles are varied and interesting (as with the example of the painted turtles, above).

For instance, some species of males, notably gopher tortoises, compete with other males who may be present for the interest of females by a kind of ritualized "jousting" in which the males charge one another, retract their heads, and ram each other in the flanks.

The male gopher tortoise uses the part of its plastron that projects from below the neck (termed the "gular spur") as a lever. The object is to hook the spur under the rival's shell and overturn him, eliminating him as a competitor until he rights himself (which could take considerable time). As indicated, these fights are ritualistic, and turtles rarely injure each other.

That's not always the case, however. Some water turtles threaten each other with hissing and a menacing display of widely gaping jaws. If this doesn't suffice to frighten one or the other away, the turtles may inflict severe wounds on each other until one of them gives up and leaves the scene.

Male turtles are not always gentle with females. Some males butt females in the flanks; some bite at the female's front legs and head gently but insistently, causing the female to withdraw her head and legs, making it more difficult to close off the genital region, hence making it more accessible. Sometimes a female indicates her willingness to mate by biting back at the male.

Some box turtles and wood turtles engage in a kind of "dance" in which the male and female approach each other, face each other at a distance of a few inches, and then move their heads rhythmically in and out and from side to side, sometimes for more than an hour. Some turtles perform a variation on this ritual in which the male circles the female one or more times.

Unlike courtship rituals, mating is much more uniform: The male always mounts the female from behind. The male's tail curves underneath, and he inserts his penis (which emerges from the cloaca and is sometimes quite long) into the cloaca of the female. Aquatic turtles mate in the water, as do amphibious turtles (generally). Turtles who live on land mate either on land or in the water.

Unlike mammals and some birds (and even some lizards and snakes), turtles have no social bonds, so mating is a random act. Female turtles often mate with more than one male, and the sperm

The desert tortoise, a resident of the American Southwest. Its large, flattened forelimbs are useful for digging. Evident in this photograph is the spur the male uses in jousting. The two males charge one another and ram each other in the flanks, all in the name of courtship.

This snapping turtle has just finished digging her nest and laying her eggs. She will soon leave her nest site, never to return.

Right: A loggerhead deposits her eggs. Note the characteristic flask shape of the nest. *Far right:* This illustration clearly depicts the egg-laying process. As the egg emerges it is caught by the turtle's hind limbs and carefully lowered into the nest.

can be stored in the female's genital tract, sometimes for several years, to fertilize future clutches of eggs.

In some species, the male grips the front of the female's carapace with his front claws. Additionally, some long-necked male turtles are able to hold onto the carapace with their jaws. Because the female box turtle has such a high, domed shell, the male often falls backward and continues to mate while lying on his back, attached at the genitals. Occasionally, a male (box turtle or other species) who has fallen on his back after mating cannot right himself, and dies.

By early summer, mating reaches a peak and is completed by late summer or early fall. This is essential in temperate climates if the eggs are to mature and hatch before winter sets in.

NEST-BUILDING AND EGG-LAYING

After mating, females seek the appropriate place to dig out a nest. For sea turtles, this is sometimes a specific, distant beach to which the female must swim. Land turtles dig nests in soil, sand, or decaying piles of leaves and other organic matter.

All turtles dig the same sort of nest: Without looking, they scoop out a flask-shaped hole as deep as their fully extended hind feet and carefully lay the eggs, which emerge from the cloaca. Tortoises living in dry climates have a difficult time excavating the ground to lay eggs; to assist themselves, they have bodily reserves of water contained in twin anal sacs. In some tortoises, these sacs are large enough to fill half the body cavity. As a female tortoise is digging her nest, she can release water from these sacs all at once or a little at a time to soften the ground and make digging easier.

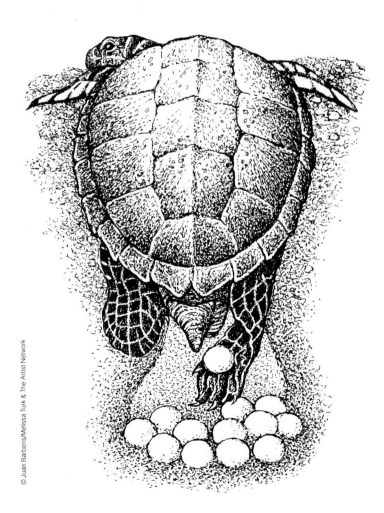

An egg emerges from the cloacal opening of a box turtle.

Turtles are frequently quite oblivious to what's going on around them while they're laying eggs. When sea turtles crawl up on the beach and dig their nests in tropical beaches, they are sometimes followed by food-gathering natives, who position themselves behind the turtles and collect the eggs before they hit the sand.

After laying the eggs, the female sometimes arranges them in the nest, then covers them with sand, soil, etc., to camouflage and protect them. When she is finished, the female leaves the nest site, never to return.

THE TURTLE EGG

Turtle eggs are white, but they vary according to species in size, shape, number, shell texture, and incubation period.

Turtle eggs vary less in size than do the adult turtles from which they come. The smallest turtle eggs are slightly smaller than an inch (2.5 centimeters) in diameter, the largest slightly smaller than three inches (8 centimeters).

Different species of turtles lay different numbers of eggs; some pancake tortoises and mud turtles lay but one egg; gopher tortoises lay up to ten; medium-sized and large land tortoises lay from ten to thirty; and green turtles, loggerheads, and hawksbills may lay more than 100.

These figures are generalizations: There are no reliable average number of eggs per species, and sometimes closely related species lay very different numbers of eggs. The largest recorded number of eggs in a single clutch belonged to a hawksbill: 242 eggs. In general, smaller turtles lay smaller and fewer eggs per clutch. A female may lay from five to ten clutches of eggs per year.

Turtle eggs vary in shape from spherical (the eggs of the snapping turtle resemble ping-pong balls) to elongated, almost cylindrical (characteristic of certain freshwater and amphibious turtles).

In general, turtles that produce the most eggs (usually marine, river, and other large turtles) also lay soft-shelled, leathery eggs, and turtles that lay only a few eggs lay eggs with hard shells. Also, those eggs with long incubation periods (typically laid by land tortoises living in hot, dry regions) are usually hard-shelled.

Turtle eggs vary, too, in their incubation period, or the time required for them to hatch. The minimum recorded natural hatching period was thirty days for the egg of a Chinese soft-shelled turtle. For more information on incubation periods, see below.

Like all reptile eggs, the turtle egg, which has existed unchanged for 100 million years, is a complex means of nourishing and protecting the baby turtle within.

Turtle eggs have several important parts. In the center is the embryo, attached by an umbilical stalk to the yellow yolk sac, its primary food supply (composed of sugars, starches, fats, and proteins). Blood vessels in the lining of the yolk sac carry the nutrients to the abdomen of the embryo. (A sea turtle's egg is 55 percent yolk, compared to 33 percent for a hen's egg.)

The amniotic sac, an envelope filled with fluid that cushions the embryo from shock and protects it from impurities, surrounds both the embryo and the yolk. As the embryo grows it gives off waste products, which would destroy it if they were not eliminated.

INSIDE THE SHELL

A snapper deposits her eggs.

Overleaf: A common snapping turtle digging her nest.

TYPICAL INCUBATION PERIODS

Time Period	Type of Turtle or Tortoise
60 days	Wood turtles, many terrapins, Australian short-necked turtles
90 days	Snapping turtles, map turtles, painted turtles
150 days	Common Australian snake-necked turtle, gopher tortoises, Galapagos tortoises
250 days	Flat tortoises
365 days or more	African bowsprit tortoises, giant snake-necked turtles

The longest recorded incubation period was 540 days, for the egg of a leopard tortoise.

In mammals, this toxic waste is dissolved and carried away through the mother's bloodstream. In turtles, the waste is transformed into insoluble uric acid, and is stored in the allantois, a sac surrounding the embryo, yolk sac, and amniotic sac. As the embryo grows and the yolk sac shrinks, the allantois gets larger as it fills with wastes; it is also a conveyor for incoming oxygen and outgoing carbon dioxide.

A final envelope, the chorion, surrounds the allantois, amniotic sac, yolk sac, and embryo; it is a tough, resilient membrane closely associated with the eggshell that contains egg white, or albumen (40 percent of a sea turtle egg, compared to 56 percent in a hen's egg). The chorion supplies the embryo with water and some food.

By weight, the shell makes up only 5 percent of the sea turtle's egg, compared with 11 percent in a hen's egg. As these percentages suggest, the turtle's shell is thinner and semipermeable, and necessary gases and moisture are able to pass through it to the embryo inside.

SEX DETERMINATION, EARLY GROWTH, AND HATCHING

Over a number of years, different observers noticed that the ratio of females to males in natural populations and in those raised in captivity varied widely for a given species, and there was apparently no way to account for the difference.

For instance, one observer noted that 81 percent of a natural population of seventy diamondback terrapins were males; another observer noted that of 1,300 diamondbacks raised in captivity, only 19 percent were males.

Recent experiments indicate that the most important factor in determining the sex ratios of many species seems to be incubation temperature. Studies of snapping turtles, pond turtles, gopher tortoises, and mud and musk turtles reveal that if the eggs are incubated at a temperature close to either limit of the range suitable for egg development, the hatchlings will be exclusively or predominantly of the same sex.

For instance, experiments showed that for many varieties of turtles, eggs incubated at the lower acceptable temperature limit (82°F, or 27°C) produced mostly males, while those incubated at the upper limit (93°F, or 34°C) were mostly female. With other varieties, the principle remained the same, but the results were reversed. Further experiments demonstrated that the middle third of the incubation period is the critical period in which temperature determines the sex ratio of the eggs.

As might be expected, in a turtle's early embryonic development, the formation of the shell plays a dominant role. It first appears as a raised section in the back of the embryo. Called the anlage, it expands outward in every direction. As it does so, it forces the turtle's ribs to remain straight, adapting to its contours. Furthermore, the shell's development determines that the turtle's growth will be mostly sideways instead of up-and-down, the direction in which most reptiles grow. This produces the turtle's typical low, flattened body type.

As indicated, the period of incubation for turtle eggs is dependent on the genetic programming of the turtles involved, as well as on a

This series of photographs captures a Florida gopher tortoise hatching. The process may take several hours or days.

© Manny Rubio

© Manny Rubio

number of environmental conditions, among them temperature, humidity, and the dampness of the soil, sand, or other vegetation in the nest.

The incubation period of a nest of snapping turtle eggs, for example, may vary from fifty-five to 125 days. Assuming a period of twenty weeks, or 140 days, between the laying of the eggs and their hatching, the snapper embryo's development might proceed something like this: At four weeks the embryo is just recognizable as an animal form; by six weeks, the tail and limbs are formed and the eyes are prominent; by eight weeks, the shell is clearly recognizable. By twelve weeks, the shell is the dominant part of the snapper's anatomy, and its fingers and toes have formed. The shell is divided into shields, and pigmentation is beginning to develop. By nineteen weeks, the fully formed baby turtle, with claws and what looks to be an oversized head, is ready to hatch.

As the embryo grows into a fully developed hatchling, the shell that has offered nourishment and protection becomes a kind of prison from which the baby turtle must escape. This it does by means of an "egg tooth," which is not a tooth at all but a horny projection located on the tip of the snout. Using the egg tooth to pierce the shell, the baby turtle then pulls it apart with its forelimbs. (The egg tooth disappears as the turtle grows.)

Because all the eggs in a nest are subject to virtually the same circumstances, they all develop at very nearly the same rate. So, once a nest of eggs starts to hatch, the eggs all hatch at about the same time.

Hatching may take several hours or even days. If the weather is too cold (in temperate climates such as the United States, for example) baby turtles may remain in their eggs over the winter, hibernating, emerging in the spring.

Herpetologist Archie Carr pointed out in his classic work on sea turtles, *So Excellent A Fishe,* that baby turtles don't break loose from

BREAKING OUT

© Manny Rubio   © Manny Rubio

the nest individually. Experiments in which eggs are isolated have shown that very few turtles—perhaps one-third—break free on their own. The rest perish.

In a nest with many eggs, the hatchlings stay in the nest until a number, maybe a dozen, have hatched. Then, in what Carr terms the actions of "a simple-minded, cooperative brotherhood," the baby turtles scrape down the walls and ceiling of their nest, urging each other to break free in what amounts to a small eruption.

Once they break free, some species have a more difficult time than others. Sea turtle hatchlings, for instance, face an especially unenviable situation.

Picture the scene: a warm, tropical beach. A hundred or more tiny turtles, only a couple of inches long, break free from a sandy nest and somehow know they're supposed to scramble headlong—a hundred feet or a hundred yards—in a stampede to the sea. And in some way not fully understood, they know which direction that is.

And what's waiting for them when they break through the sand? Perhaps nothing, but that's not often the case. As Carr says, "the whole world seems against the hatchlings both during their trip from the nest to the surf and for an unknown time after they enter the sea."

Apart from humans (most of whom are interested in eggs rather than baby turtles), significant predators include dogs, buzzards,

A great many hatchlings don't make it. Animals and humans destroy countless turtle nests every year.

skunks, hawks, opossums, wild pigs, and coyotes. Many of these animals seem particularly adept at knowing when the eggs are laid and when they will hatch.

How many sea turtles make it across the beach to the surf? In many cases, certainly, a minority of those that emerge from the nest—maybe a dozen out of a hundred. And for those that make it, the safety of their first weeks and months in the ocean are threatened by gulls, large fish, and so on. All turtles face at least one additional obstacle: When they hatch, their shells are not fully hardened, making them more susceptible to predators.

Of course, many turtle nests are destroyed long before the baby turtles are ready to hatch. Because sea turtles return to the same beaches to lay eggs (and because they often show up by the hundreds or thousands), humans and other predators are there waiting to break into the nests for the turtle eggs, which they eat or extract the oil from.

The problems of sea turtle nests are not isolated, only perhaps the most well-publicized: Studies of snapping turtle nests have shown that between one-half and three-fourths are routinely destroyed, sometimes by humans but more frequently by mammals such as raccoons, opossums, dogs, wildcats, and bears.

Little is known of the first year or so of the lives of most hatchlings in the wild: They simply disappear from sight. We know that most have the capacity to go weeks or months without eating, if necessary. The next time most turtles (marine, amphibious, or land) appear in the wild is as adults a year or more old.

Most records of turtle life are based on studies of adult turtles, and most of these studies mention the absence of juvenile or adolescent turtles among adult populations. This may mean that pre-adult turtles live in different environments from those environments inhabited by adults—perhaps those offering the promise of more anonymity and protection.

This conclusion is supported, for instance, by what is known of the wood turtle's diet: Juveniles prefer meat (insects, worms, etc.), suggesting that they spend their time in the hospitable environs of marshes, bogs, and streams, where such creatures are found.

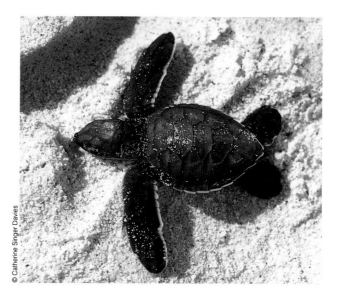

A hatchling green turtle, which died shortly after this photo was taken.

GROWTH

It's hard to accurately generalize about how rapidly turtles grow and mature. Depending on the species, turtles reach sexual maturity and full size at a variety of ages, and rates of growth are nonuniform throughout a turtle's life.

Smaller species usually reach sexual maturity and full size earliest. Male pond sliders, for instance, are sexually mature between two and five years of age; snapping turtles reach sexual maturity at six to eight years of age and continue to grow in size into their teens; common box turtles, which may live for more than 100 years, continue to grow into their twenties.

Fairly accurate records have been kept of the size and weight of many common species of turtles, but it's difficult to correlate this with a turtle's age because the life histories of very few turtles have been documented from birth.

As is the case with reptiles generally, baby turtles look and act very much like adults. However, if you were to examine a baby turtle shortly after it hatches, you'd notice two things that distinguish it from an adult. First, all baby turtles have an umbilical scar in the middle of the plastron; this looks somewhat like a human belly button, and disappears within the first year. Second, a baby turtle sometimes has a different shape, color, or different proportions from an adult of the same species.

Often, the differences are shell-related. Pancake tortoises, for example, have flat shells as adults but curved shells as juveniles. The shell of the Kemp's ridley, a sea turtle, becomes wider and wider as it matures; the shells of some adults are wider than they are long. Young leatherbacks have a mosaic pattern on their shells that completely disappears as they get older.

A turtle's shell grows from a layer of cells between the two layers of the carapace; the direction of the growth is outward from the center

Galapagos tortoises survive longer than any other member of the Testudinae family; some have been known to live for 150 years.

of each plate or scute. Close examination of the plates may reveal "growth rings" corresponding to phases of growth, much like those in trees. These sometimes become smooth and indistinct as a turtle gets older.

In some land tortoises, the shape of the shell changes with age. In many, the smooth scutes along the rim of the shell become wavy or start to flare or turn upward with age. In older painted turtles, longitudinal furrows often develop across the borders of the carapacial plates, and the "humps" or "saddles" on giant Galapagos tortoises only develop later in life.

BEHAVIOR CHANGES

From the time they hatch until they die, most of a turtle's actions are based on instinct, which might be defined as prepatterned behavior. A baby turtle never knows its mother, and although turtles are capable of learning, it would seem that they use their instinct rather than intellect in order to survive.

In captivity, groups of turtles have been observed to form themselves into a sort of primitive hierarchy in which some will defer to others; but, except for courtship and mating, most turtles have no relations with other turtles. There's no evidence that they communicate with one another or even acknowledge the existence of each other. For example, a semiaquatic turtle in an aquarium, in an effort to get where it wants to go, will attempt to climb over or swim past another turtle as if it's simply a rock or a log.

LONGEVITY

Except for the interest in a turtle's shell, people are more fascinated with a turtle's longevity than any other chelonian characteristic. It's true that given a favorable habitat and fortunate circumstances, many species of turtles live a long time.

Still, the longevity of turtles is a subject about which we have only a limited amount of information. As Archie Carr said in *Handbook of Turtles,* "The only reliable means of gaining an idea of how long turtles live is to live with them, and this of course can become monotonous in the extreme."

Emydid turtles—freshwater and semiaquatic species such as red-eared sliders, box turtles, wood turtles, map turtles, diamondback terrapins, and pond turtles—have a lifespan anywhere from twenty years (estimated, painted turtle) to forty-two years (recorded, spotted turtle) to fifty-eight (recorded, wood turtle) to 100 plus (recorded, common box turtle).

The second-largest turtle family, Testudinae (tortoises), contains some especially long-lived members: European land tortoises have been recorded to live for more than 120 years, and Galapagos tortoises have lived for more than 150 years.

In general, larger, slower-developing species have longer lifespans, but to attribute longevity to the chelonians as a whole is a mistake, the stuff of folklore and superstition: By human standards, most turtles only live a relatively short period of time.

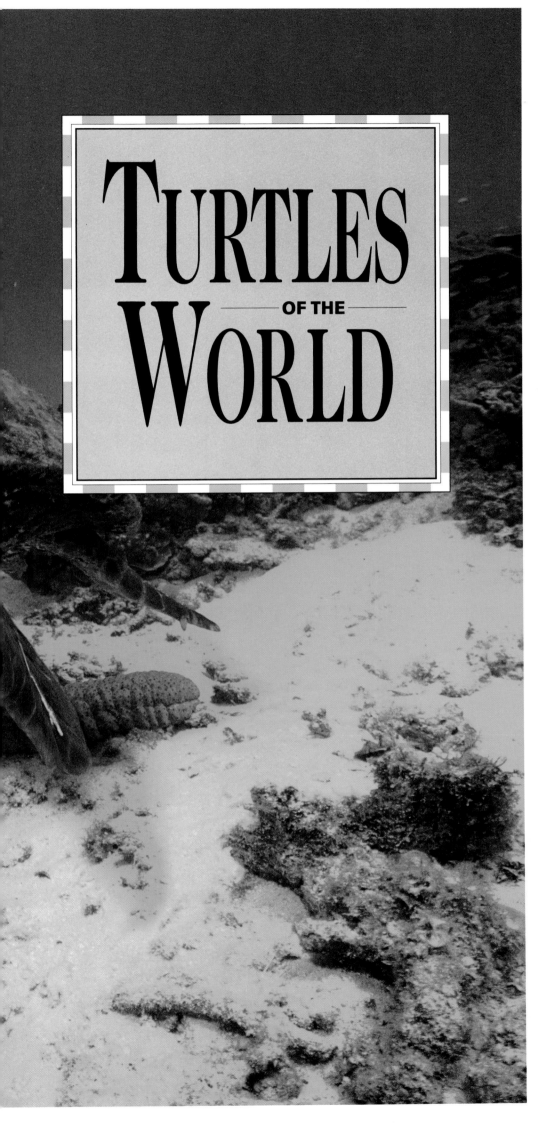

TURTLES
OF THE
WORLD

Herpetologists don't agree completely on one single classification system for turtles. In fact, Pritchard's *Encyclopedia of Turtles,* one of the most authoritative and comprehensive works on turtles, lists six different (though not mutually exclusive) forms of classification by modern authorities. These systems separate turtles into groups based on a number of categories: order, suborder, infraorder, superfamily, and family. For our purposes, however, categorization will be more basic and relatively simple.

As stated earlier, most turtles of the world fall into the suborder Cryptodira, the distinguishing feature of which is that they draw their necks straight back into their shells. The majority of this book, and this section in particular, will be devoted to a description of straight-necked turtles.

Most authorities separate straight-necked turtles into seven distinct families: Chelydridae, snapping turtles; Kinosternidae, mud and musk turtles; Trionychidae, soft-shell turtles; Emydidae, semiaquatic turtles; Testudinidae, tortoises; Chelonidae, sea turtles; and Dermochelyidae, leatherback turtles.

Several of these families have certain characteristics in common, so in this book they will be treated as five groups: snapping, mud and musk turtles; soft-shell turtles; semiaquatic turtles; tortoises; and marine turtles (sea turtles and leatherback turtles).

A few turtles belong to the suborder Pleurodira, or side-necked turtles, which means that they lay their necks and heads sideways in the groove between the carapace and plastron (upper and lower parts of the shell). At the end of the sections on straight-necked turtles, I will describe a few of the more prominent side-necked turtles.

It's neither possible nor desirable in a book of this size and scope to describe the majority of the 200-plus species of turtles living. For readers interested in a really complete description of turtle species, I recommend *Handbook of Turtles* by Archie Carr; *Turtles of the United States* by Ernst and Barbour; *Turtles, Tortoises and Terrapins* by Fritz Obst; and *Encyclopedia of Turtles* by Peter Pritchard.

Instead, I'll discuss the turtles that are most representative of a particular family and those of a specific type that are most numerous or widespread.

SNAPPING, MUD, AND MUSK TURTLES

Snapping, mud, and musk turtles are grouped together because they share several characteristics: All live in the Western Hemisphere, largely in freshwater aquatic conditions (ponds, lakes, rivers, and streams); their coloration is generally unattractive and drab, and many species have aggressive temperaments.

The alligator snapper *(Macroclemys temmincki)* lies motionless on the bottom of streams, ponds, and lakes with its mouth open. Its tongue appears to be a red, wriggling worm, and unsuspecting fish looking for a meal become the snapper's prey.

© Dr. G.J. Chafaris

SNAPPING TURTLES

Some people think that snapping turtles are big, mean, and ugly. Well, they're big: A large common snapping turtle gets to be almost 3 feet (1 meter) long from its aggressive snout to the tip of its tail and weighs about 50 pounds (19 kilograms) (the heaviest one on record, fattened in a swill barrel, tipped the scales at 86 pounds [32 kilograms]). Alligator snappers are even bigger.

Snappers are aggressive, too. They're ready to bite right out of the egg, and their disposition worsens with age. If captured, they're initially aggressively hostile; later, they may become withdrawn, but they lose none of their meanness.

But ugly? Well, it's true that beauty is in the eye of the beholder, but snapping turtles have a kind of awe-inspiring appeal, not unlike that possessed by a heavyweight boxer or an Army tank: They're so good, so ruthlessly efficient, at what they do. And if you're smart, you don't mess with them.

The Alligator Snapping Turtle

There are two recognized species of snapping turtle: the alligator snapper (*Macroclemys temmincki*) and the common snapper (*Chelydra serpentina*). The larger of the two is the alligator snapper, which probably derives its name from the fact that the three prominent ridges on its carapace and its long tail give it an appearance similar to that of an alligator. Another source of its name may come from a folktale stating that the alligator snapper came into being when an ordinary snapping turtle mated with an alligator.

The alligator snapper is found mostly in the southern Mississippi River valley from Kansas, Missouri, Illinois, and Iowa, south to the Gulf of Mexico. It extends west into parts of Texas and Oklahoma and east, into Kentucky, Tennessee, Alabama, Georgia, and Florida. It lives, for the most part, in the deep waters of rivers, canals, and lakes.

Not much is known of the alligator snapper's behavior, but it is believed to be nocturnal and quite sedentary. It generally crawls along the bottom instead of swimming. The diet of alligator snappers is mostly meat—it

© Dr. E.R. Degginger

eats living and dead fish, frogs, snakes, turtles, crayfish, mussels, and snails—and an occasional aquatic plant.

Sometimes the alligator snapper waits in ambush for food rather than foraging for it. To do this, it makes use of one of the most unusual methods of acquiring food in the animal kingdom: The snapper lies motionless on the bottom with only its mouth open, its brownish, algae-covered shell providing the perfect camouflage. In the center of the floor of the alligator snapper's mouth is a double-ended, movable section of its tongue that looks like a wriggling, red worm. Fish are frequently attracted to this "bait" and are quickly devoured when they get within range of *Macroclemys'* hooked beak.

Except for sea turtles, the alligator snapper is the largest North American turtle and one of the largest freshwater turtles in the world. Males grow to a much greater size than females: A big male might have a shell 2 feet (60 centimeters) long, plus another foot each for the head and tail. Such a turtle

could easily weigh 150 pounds (56 kilograms); alligator snappers have been recorded at more than 200 pounds (75 kilograms). Other distinctive physical features of *Macroclemys temmincki* include eyes on the side of the head that cannot be seen from directly above; a very wide head that can only be withdrawn a little way; large, bulky legs equipped with sharp claws; a similar appearance for both males and females; and a smaller plastron shaped like a cross.

Alligator snappers lay an average of about twenty-five eggs per clutch; it is thought that females may not lay eggs every year, and if they do, they lay only a single clutch. The typical lifespan for an alligator snapper is about fifty years, though some have been known to live longer. Adult alligator snappers have no enemies except man; younger turtles are probably killed by alligators, and the nests are raided by raccoons and skunks. The meat of the alligator snapper is eaten in the southern United States, though it is not as popular as that of the common snapper.

From this perspective, it's easy to see the resemblance between an alligator snapper and its namesake.

The Common Snapping Turtle

The common snapping turtle is far more abundant and has a range much greater than that of the alligator snapper. It is found all across the United States and southern Canada from the East Coast to the Rocky Mountains; it extends south into Mexico, Central America, and a few of the northern countries of South America. There are four subspecies in all; three differ in minor ways from the most prevalent, *Chelydra serpentina serpentina*.

Common snappers live mostly in bodies of water with marshy or muddy banks. They are active primarily at night; although essentially aquatic, they occasionally venture out onto land for considerable distances. When in the water, snappers usually crawl on the bottom, though they are good swimmers. Sometimes they bask half-submerged.

In the wintertime, snappers in North America burrow into the muddy bottom and hibernate. Now and again, they settle beneath submerged trees or in muskrat burrows, sometimes in large groups. By late October, most have become inactive, emerging again in March, April, or May. Apparently, common snappers tolerate cold weather fairly well; some have been seen crawling on and beneath ice.

The common snapper is omnivorous; its diet is similar to that of the alligator snapper, though it probably eats more vegetable matter, and it's quick enough to catch waterfowl from below the surface.

As is true of alligator snappers, common snappers have large, muscular legs, feet equipped with thick, sharp claws, and a long, ridged tail. Common snappers are smaller than alligator snappers, and their shells are flatter and their necks are longer. It's safe to pick up an alligator snapper by gripping it on the carapace, behind its head, but if you try that with an ordinary snapper, it will turn its head in a flash and bite your hand.

The best way to pick up any sort of snapping turtle is by its rear legs, holding the turtle far out from your body to avoid its jaws. Do not pick up a snapper by its tail—doing so will cause a potentially fatal injury to the turtle. When they're first picked up, snappers will often emit a foul-smelling musk from their tail region.

In fifteen to twenty years the hatchling snapper will approach the size of the adult.

© John F. O'Connor/PhotoNats

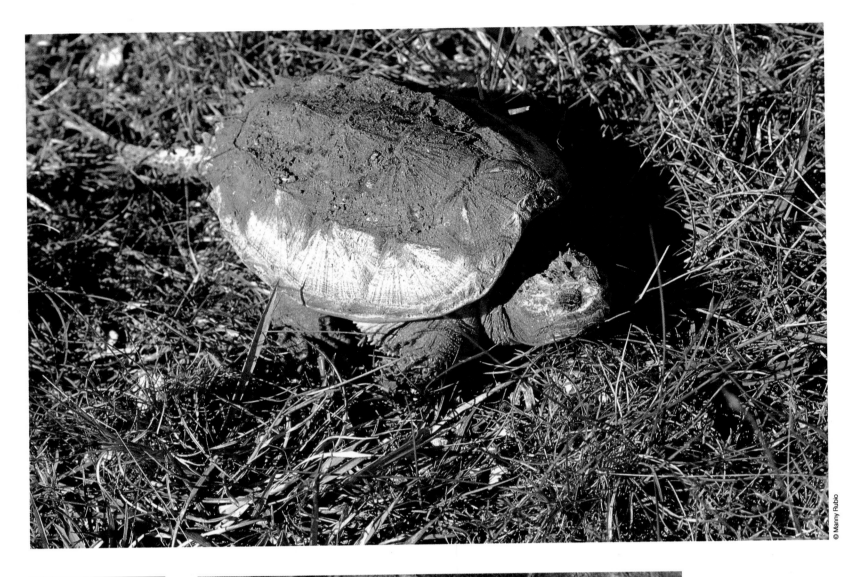

Above: The Florida snapping turtle *(Chelydra serpentina osceola),* a subspecies of the common snapper.
Right: A closeup of the head of an adult common snapping turtle *(Chelydra serpentina serpentina).* Note the large, powerful claws.

Female snappers lay eggs at least once a season, sometimes more. Like the alligator snapper, the common snapper's carapace is drab in color—olive-brown, dark brown, or nearly black—and algae often grow on the shells of adults. The small plastron is tan or yellow and lacks markings.

Common snappers are extraordinarily aggressive turtles. They strike "with the speed and power of a big rattlesnake," says Archie Carr, at anything near them. This is especially true on land, where a snapper often lunges with such force that its body is lifted off the ground and carried forward.

This isn't to say that snappers seek out victims to attack. In the water, snappers are less belligerent and often prefer to escape what they perceive as danger. Snappers never become truly tame in captivity and, although hardy, make poor pets.

Snapping turtle shells had widespread ceremonial use among Native Americans, according to Carr. Snappers can be caught on fishing lines, and in North America, common snapper meat is probably the most widely eaten turtle meat and is often considered a delicacy. The eggs, too, are frequently eaten, although they will not hard-boil.

MUD AND MUSK TURTLES

The family Kinosternidae consists of small, aquatic turtles that live in North and Central America. They are known popularly as mud and musk turtles, and they number about twenty to twenty-five species in all. Most of these turtles belong to one of two genera: *Kinosternon* (mud turtles) and *Sternotherus* (musk turtles).

Most mud and musk turtles are small, having carapace lengths of 4 to 7 inches (10 to 18 centimeters); unlike snapping turtles, their tails are always short. Most species have short tubercles of barbels (projections) under their chins and on their throats. Mud and musk turtles have a hinged plastron, which allows some of them to close off their shell openings completely, protecting their head, limbs, and tail. In general, their shells are smooth, unmarked, and dark-colored (olive, brown, or black). All four of their feet are webbed.

© Dr. E.R. Degginger

There are about a dozen species of mud turtles, only a few of which will be discussed in detail. The most widespread in the United States is the common mud turtle (*Kinosternon subrubum*), which consists of three subspecies, popularly known as the eastern mud turtle, the Florida mud turtle, and the Mississippi mud turtle. Taken together, these three turtles are found mostly in the southeastern United States: South Carolina, Georgia, Alabama, Mississippi, Arkansas, Louisiana, and parts of New Jersey, Maryland, Pennsylvania, Delaware, Virginia, North Carolina, Illinois, Indiana, Kentucky, Tennessee, Oklahoma, and Texas.

The mud turtle prefers to live in shallow, slow-moving, or still bodies of water with soft bottoms, such as ponds, marshes, canals, or drainage ditches. It spends a good deal of time crawling about on the bottom, but sometimes floats near the surface and even prowls about on land. It rarely basks. On both land and water, however, mud turtles travel relatively short distances.

The common mud turtle is omnivorous, eating insects, carrion, algae, mollusks, fish, and aquatic vegetation. In winter, the species hibernates in mud, decayed wood, or vegetable debris. In the southern reaches of its range, the mud turtle remains active year round.

The razorback musk turtle *(Sternotherus carinatus)*, the largest of the genus, reaches a maximum length of about 6 inches (15 cm).

The striped-neck musk turtle *(Sternotherus minorpeltifer)* is a highly aquatic species living in the American South.

Nesting females show a peculiarity: They begin digging their nest with their front feet, then turn and complete it with their hind legs. They lay very few eggs, two to five are typical, and a single egg is not uncommon. Nests are relatively shallow, and the turtles make comparatively little effort to cover the eggs and conceal the nest once they are finished laying them.

The disposition of mud turtles varies; some are docile, but others are mean-tempered and bite savagely. Peter Pritchard says the most painful turtle bite he ever received was from a male Florida mud turtle. Newly captured specimens frequently emit a foul-smelling secretion. Once they become used to captivity, however, mud turtles usually cease both biting and giving off this smelly liquid. Mud turtles have a fairly long lifespan: One female, captured as an adult, lived for thirty-eight years.

Other North American mud turtles include the yellow, Sonoran, and striped mud turtles. The first two are found in the southwestern United States; the latter is found chiefly in peninsular Florida.

Another species, the white-lipped mud turtle, has a wide, entirely tropical range, and is found from Veracruz on the Gulf of Mexico south to Guatemala and northwest Colombia and Ecuador. Its appearance is

distinguished most notably by the coloring of its head: The top and sides are dark brown, but the jaws and underside of the neck are white, including the upper and lower "lip" area.

White-lipped mud turtles are semiaquatic rather than aquatic. Reproduction occurs throughout the year, though females often lay only one egg. No real nest is made; sometimes the egg or eggs simply are covered with decaying leaves or vegetable matter. This variety of mud turtle is abundant throughout its range and though small (4 to 5 inches [10 to 13 centimeters] being typical), it is an important source of food in tropical Mexico and Nicaragua.

Other Central and South American mud turtles include the scorpion mud turtle and the red-cheeked mud turtle.

Musk turtles are closely related and similar in appearance and habits to mud turtles, but are generally smaller. There are fewer species of musk turtles than mud turtles, about eight in all, but they make their presence powerfully felt because of the nauseating fluid they emit from their musk glands when first handled. (Carr said: "I find the . . . musk [of the mud turtle] rather nauseating, though far from being as utterly revolting as the stench that exudes from a hysterical stink-jim.")

Additionally, many musk turtles are initially ill-tempered, scratching and biting their handler viciously. As is the case with mud turtles, however, musk turtles become quite tame in captivity.

In the United States, the most representative species is the common musk turtle (*Sternotherus odoratus*), popularly known as the stinkpot or stinkjim. It is easily identified by light stripes on the side of its head and neck. Its range extends across most of the United States east of the Mississippi River and the eastern two-thirds of Texas.

The common musk turtle is highly aquatic and, unlike the mud turtle, is frequently found in deep bodies of water. Carr observed musk turtles walking on the bottom of clear springs in Florida that were thirty feet (nine meters) deep. Other North American musk turtle species include the razorback and the loggerhead musk turtle, both of which inhabit only southern states.

Two musk turtles found in southern Mexico and Central America (genus *Stauroty-*

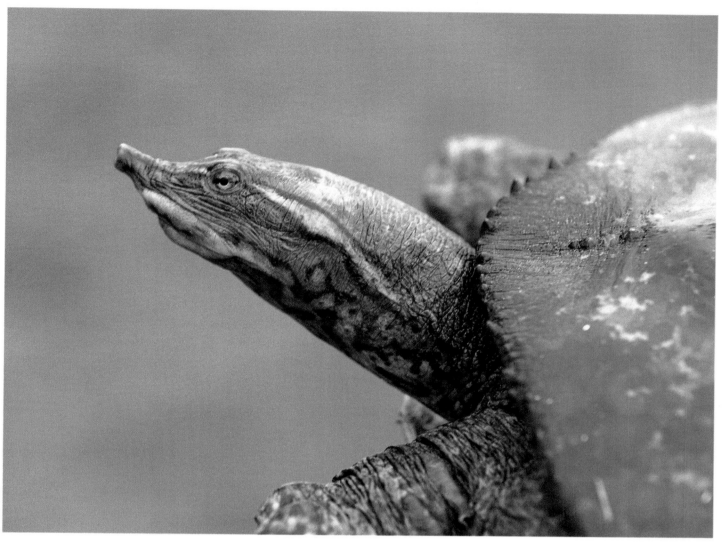

© A.B. Sheldon

pus), the guau turtle and crucilla turtle, are worth noting because of their relatively large size. Termed "giant" musk turtles, they are commonly a foot (30 centimeters) in length.

SOFT-SHELL TURTLES

Unlike snappers and mud and musk turtles, soft-shell turtles are predominantly fresh-water aquatic turtles found all over the world. Six genera and twenty-three species live in North America, Southeast Asia, Africa, and the Middle East.

Soft-shell turtles vary greatly in size and disposition, but many of their habits are similar, and their appearance is unmistakable. With their large, flattened, nearly circular carapaces and pointed, inquisitive-looking snouts, they seem, as Pritchard says, like animated pancakes. The family name, Trionychidae, refers not to their shells, however, but instead to the fact that soft-shell turtles have only three claws on each foot.

© John Cancalosi/Tom Stack & Associates

Above, top: A closeup of the head of the spiny soft-shell *(Trionyx spiniferus),* the most common of North American soft-shell turtles. Soft-shells are known for their aggressiveness. *Above, bottom:* A turtle that obtains food as both a predator and scavenger, the spiny soft-shell is capable of moving quickly both on land and in water.

The Florida soft-shell (*Trionyx ferox*), the largest of the North American soft-shells, grows to a carapace length of 20 inches (51 cm).

The term "soft-shell" is somewhat of a misnomer, for the shells of soft-shell turtles merely lack horny plates, not rigidity. The carapace of soft-shells only appears soft, because it is flat and covered with a leathery skin. The bones underneath are often quite thick; only the rim of the turtle's carapace is flexible.

The underside of soft-shells is also distinctive; in most, the plastron extends quite far forward, matching the outline of the cara-pace above or extending slightly beyond it, providing protection for the head and front limbs. At the hind feet, however, the plastron seems to be cut away, extending perhaps two-thirds the length of the carapace and leaving most of the turtle's legs and tail exposed. In most soft-shells, it is not merely the external surface of the plastron that is reduced—there are also large boneless areas in the plastron's internal structure.

Most soft-shells are highly aquatic and are

agile, strong swimmers. Typically, soft-shells have webbed feet. They have very sharp jaws, and like snappers, they strike their prey swiftly and with power. Soft-shells also are capable of moving rapidly on land: Ernst and Barbour state that a North American smooth soft-shell turtle (*Trionyx muticus*) is capable of outdistancing a human being on a level, unobstructed surface.

In general, soft-shells are medium- to large-sized turtles. At the small end of the continuum, a male smooth soft-shell, which lives in the central United States, might grow to a carapace length of 7 inches (18 centimeters); at the other end of the spectrum, the largest of the soft-shells, the Indian soft-shell (*Chitra indica*) might have a carapace length of 5 feet (1.5 meters).

As is the case with many species, female soft-shells are often considerably larger than males. One of the easiest means of differentiating the sexes is to examine the tail: Males have thick, long tails; the female's is usually short, sometimes not reaching the edge of the carapace.

Soft-shells have elongated, narrow skulls and long, flexible necks. This allows them to burrow in the mud of shallow ponds and streams, merely extending their nostrils to the surface to breathe. The skin of many soft-shells is more water permeable than that of other turtles; therefore, soft-shells are able to take in oxygen by means of gaseous exchange through the skin and lining of the throat, in addition to normal breathing. Soft-shells lack cloacal sacs, however, and cannot engage in anal respiration.

Many soft-shells are quite aggressive (*ferox,* the Latin name for the Florida soft-shell, means "wild" or "savage"), so their long necks also enable them to easily reach around and bite anyone attempting to capture or pick them up.

An efficient way to capture soft-shells buried in the mud Carr (citing the master's thesis of Lewis Marchand) reports, is to "thrust the hand into the mud until the carapace is felt, then to slide the hand forward until the anterior margin of the shell is reached. The fingers are then gently slipped around the animal's neck, and when a secure hold has been obtained, all possible pressure is applied and the turtle is pulled up through the water and thrown into the boat...a vigorous choking grip may be necessary to discourage attempts at biting." Definitely a procedure best left to the dedicated turtle enthusiast!

Most species (sixteen) of soft-shell turtles belong to the genus *Trionyx* and are found, among other places, in the United States, Mexico, most of Africa, Syria, Iraq, India, Burma, China, Japan, Taiwan, and Vietnam. In countries other than the United States, the habits of the soft-shell turtle frequently are little known, because the principal interest people have in it is as a source of food.

In North America, the most common soft-shell turtle is the spiny soft-shell (*Trionyx spinifer*), which gets its name from tiny, conical projections along the anterior (front) margins of the carapace. There are currently six recognized subspecies of the spiny soft-shell. In the United States, it lives throughout most of the eastern, central, and southern states; its range extends west to the

© Dr. E.R. Degginger

Rocky Mountains, across Texas and into the Southwest. In Canada, it is found in southern Quebec and Ontario; in Mexico for 100 to 200 miles (160 to 320 kilometers) south of the Mexico-United States border.

The spiny soft-shell is a medium- to large-sized soft-shell turtle whose leathery shell has a sandpaper-like surface. Females grow to 20 inches (50 centimeters); males to 10 inches (25 centimeters). The color of its shell ranges from olive to tan, with a pattern of dark ocelli (circular markings, often with dark centers) or blotches and one or two dark lines around the margin; the plastron is an unmarked white or yellow; its head has two light stripes with dark borders on the side.

Spiny soft-shells live in a variety of watery habitats with soft bottoms and aquatic vegetation: marshes, creeks, ponds, bayous, rivers, and lakes. They spend most of their time foraging for food at the surface or, as men-

tioned above, buried in the bottom with only their heads and necks protruding. Spiny soft-shells are primarily carnivorous, eating crayfish, insects, earthworms, fish, tadpoles, and frogs. Sometimes they swim along the bottom, feeding in what appears to be a random fashion; at other times, they deliberately pursue prey or lie in ambush waiting for it.

As do many other aquatic turtles in the Western Hemisphere, soft-shells in northern

The eastern spiny soft-shell (*Trionyx spiniferus spiniferus*), a subspecies that lives east of the Mississippi River and as far south as northern Alabama.

areas hibernate underwater from November to April; in southern areas, they are active all year. Nests are usually built in June or July; clutches average twenty hard-shelled, brittle eggs slightly larger than 1 inch (2.5 centimeters) in diameter. Raccoons and skunks raid their nests, and fish, other turtles, snakes, birds, and mammals eat the young. The only threat to adults are alligators and human beings. There is evidence that the spiny soft-shell can live to be sixty years of age or older.

Five species of soft-shell turtles are found in Africa, most of them quite large. The Nubian soft-shell, Aubrey's soft-shell, and the Zambesi soft-shell may all reach a carapace length of more than 2 feet (60 centimeters); the Nile soft-shell may grow to a carapace length of more than 3 feet (90 centimeters). Pritchard reported a population of Nile soft-shell turtles living in six to fifteen fathoms (eleven to twenty-eight meters) of sea water off the coast of Turkey. The animals were numerous enough to pester fishermen all along the coast, and were considered so vicious that fishermen did not like to bring them into their boats.

Six species of soft-shells live in or near India. One, the Indian flap-shelled turtle, is small (males: 6 inches [15 centimeters]; females: 11 inches [28 centimeters]) and is distinguished by its domed carapace and (in some subspecies) the yellow spots on its shell. Another species, the Indian soft-shell, is known for its great size (around 5 feet [1.5 meters] long), flipperlike feet, and the absence of a clear distinction between the anterior carapace and the neck. The shell seems to form itself into a funnel at the neck. From the end of the funnel, a small, narrow head with eyes very near the snout, emerges. Large specimens of the Indian soft-shell have been reported to attack and wreck small boats.

One species living in Bangladesh, *Trionyx nigricans,* apparently no longer exists in the wild. For more than 100 years, a semicaptive colony of these large turtles has been kept as a part of a religious shrine. Some are quite large (carapaces of about 3 feet [1 meter]) and tame, coming to feed when called.

Other species live in Burma and Malaya; the Chinese soft-shell (*Trionyx sinensis*) is found in China, Taiwan, Korea, Japan, and has even been introduced in Hawaii.

Opposite page: Painted turtles (Chrysemys picta) are found in the eastern seaboard of North America, from Nova Scotia south to northern Georgia. *Overleaf:* The yellow-bellied turtle (Chrysemys scripta) has a thick, deep, strongly sculpted carapace.

SEMIAQUATIC TURTLES

The Emydidae is the largest family of living turtles, comprising some thirty genera and eighty-five species. Emydid turtles are largely freshwater and semiterrestrial turtles: Many divide their time between land and water and spend a good deal of time basking; some, which resemble tortoises, spend most of their time on land.

Emydid turtles range in size from the 4-inch (10-centimeter) bog turtle, which lives in the United States, to the batagur turtle of Southeast Asia, which grows to a carapace length of 2 feet (60 centimeters) and may weigh 60 pounds (22 kilograms).

Most emydid turtles live in the northern hemisphere, though a few Asian species live south of the equator. Emydid turtles are found in the greatest abundance and variety in eastern North America and Southeast Asia. They also live in Central and South America and India; only a handful of species are found in Europe, Africa, and the Middle East. No emydid turtles live in Australia.

In North America, there are three distinct groups of emydid turtles: basking turtles, map turtles, and terrapins, most of which have short necks, broad jaw surfaces, and a preference for running water (rivers and streams), although many basking turtles prefer still water; pond and box turtles, which have short necks, narrow jaw surfaces, and a tendency to live on land; and chicken and Blanding's turtles, which have long necks, narrow jaw surfaces, and a preference for relatively still waters.

BASKING TURTLES, MAP TURTLES, AND TERRAPINS

Basking Turtles

Basking turtles include about fourteen species and thirty-three subspecies which are found in the southeastern and south-central United States, including Illinois, Indiana, Missouri, Kentucky, Tennessee, North and South Carolina, Georgia, Alabama, Mississippi, Arkansas, Louisiana, Oklahoma, and

Above: A closeup of a red-eared slider *(Trachemys scripta elegans). Right:* Note the red "ear patch" and highly decorative shell.

© A.B. Sheldon

chemyd turtles are known as sliders; pseudemyds as cooters and red bellies; and chrysemyds as painted turtles.

Most people would immediately recognize the genus because it includes the most widely kept pet turtle in the world, *Trachemys scripta elegans,* commonly known as the red-eared slider (because of the red patch behind its ear and its habit, in the wild, of sliding off the logs on which it frequently basks, into the water when it senses danger approaching).

Baby red-eared sliders were once raised and sold by the millions in "turtle farms" in the United States and Europe. Then, in the 1970s, salmonella infections in humans were traced to pet *Trachemys scripta elegans,* and the sale of baby sliders was prohibited. This was a blessing for the turtles, because they are quite delicate as juveniles and, because of neglect and inadvertent mistreatment, often lived no more than two months. Adult red-ears, which are much hardier animals, are still commonly available in pet stores.

Basking turtles are medium- to large-sized turtles (8 to 16 inches [20 to 41 centimeters]) that spend much of their time on logs, rocks, or banks adjacent to water, sometimes gathering in large groups. They prefer aquatic habitats with soft bottoms and abundant vegetation. Males are usually smaller than females (sometimes half the size) and are easily identified by the extremely long claws found on their front feet, which are used to stroke the female's face in courtship.

Basking turtles have oval, moderately domed carapaces, sometimes with elaborate geometrical patterns. Often the marginal plates are a bright color, such as red or yellow, that contrasts with the green, brown, or black carapace. The skin of the head and feet is generally green, olive, or black, with contrasting, longitudinal yellow stripes. Behind the eye is a red, orange, or yellow horizontal line or spot. The skin of the head is relatively smooth, while the feet are somewhat more scaly. The plastron is usually bright yellow or red, sometimes with intricate configurations in a contrasting color. As they age, the carapaces of both males and females frequently become dark, losing all color patterning.

Depending on their age, basking turtles

Texas. In addition, the genus extends into Mexico, Central America, the northwest corner of South America, southern Brazil, and northern Argentina. It is found also on the Cayman Islands, Cuba, Jamaica, Puerto Rico, and the Bahamas.

Until recently (the mid-1980s), basking turtles typically were grouped into two genera, *Pseudemys* and *Chrysemys,* the latter consisting of a single species, *Chrysemys picta,* the painted turtle. Now, a third designation, *Trachemys,* is used. Popularly, tra-

© A.B. Sheldon

A juvenile Suwanee cooter *(Pseudemys concinna suwanniencis)* basks in the sun.

prefer different sorts of food. When young, they often choose meat, but as they grow older they eat progressively larger amounts of vegetable matter. Adults are omnivorous and will eat any food available.

Typically, basking turtles are mild-mannered, preferring to retreat or escape when threatened. They are diurnal: sleeping at night, basking on logs or the water's surface from midmorning to midafternoon, and feeding mostly in the early morning and late afternoon. In late fall, basking turtles hibernate, usually underwater or in muskrat burrows, but if there is a winter warm spell, they may become temporarily active. Basking turtles normally remain in one place, near good basking and feeding sites. They

typically nest in June or July, laying about fifteen oval eggs usually more than once per season. Basking turtles are generally hardy and may live thirty years or more.

Their nests are raided by opossums, skunks, bears, and raccoons. Snakes, large wading birds, large fish, carnivorous turtles, and the above-mentioned mammals eat juveniles. Alligators, mammals, and humans eat adults, and humans destroy many more, both willfully (shooting them, running over them in cars) and through ignorance (keeping them as pets but not bothering to find out their needs). Ernst and Barbour's comment about the red-eared slider applies to the genus as a whole: "It is a marvel that the species survives."

Top: A male Texas slider *(Pseudemys texana):* Note the long claws characteristic of males.
Middle left: The hieroglyphic slider *(Pseudemys concinna heiroglyphica),* a large emydid living in the south-central states of the United States.
Middle right: The Alabama red-bellied turtle *(Pseudemys rubriventris alabamensis)* is a rare turtle found only in the vicinity of Mobile Bay, Alabama.
Bottom: The Missouri slider *(Pseudemys florida hoyi)* lives in the central United States.

Map Turtles

Map turtles (genus *Graptemys*) consist of ten species of medium-sized, highly aquatic turtles that live, for the most part, in river systems of the eastern and central United States. Five of the ten species, however, live in southern Mississippi and Alabama, and two are found only in Texas.

Map turtles get their name from the intricate patterns of yellow or cream-colored lines (resembling the lines of topographical maps) on their green or brown carapaces. Three well-known species are the common map turtle (*Graptemys geographica*), the black-knobbed sawback (*Graptemys nigrinoda*), and the false map turtle (*Graptemys pseudogeographica*).

Map turtles have striped and patterned heads and limbs, similar to painted turtles and sliders. On many species, the carapace has a ridge of pointed projections, which accounts for the nickname "sawback."

There are extreme differences, both physical and behavioral, between the sexes among map turtles. In several species females may be more than twice as large as males. For instance, the largest Barbour's map turtle (*Graptemys barbouri*) on record, a female, had a carapace length of almost 13 inches (33 centimeters); males are not known to exceed 5 inches (13 centimeters). (Females of other species range in size from 5 to 11 inches [13 to 27 centimeters], males from 4 to 6 inches [10 to 15 centimeters].)

Females also develop very large heads (the above specimen had a head 3 inches [8 centimeters] wide) with broad jaw surfaces, which they use to crush the shellfish that form a significant part of their diets. Alternately, males have small, narrow heads and jaw surfaces and are likely to eat softer animals, such as insects and worms. Both sexes eat some vegetable matter as well.

Further, males tend to be found basking in the vicinity of partially submerged tree branches and logs near the banks of rivers; females inhabit the muddy areas of river bottoms. In general, map turtles are shy and wary of danger. They do not do well in captivity.

The Alabama map turtle (*Graptemys pulchre*) is characterized by a black line along the vertebral ridge.

Map turtles are found throughout the eastern and southern United States. Many species have raised or pointed median projections, which gives rise to the common name "sawback." *Above, top:* The black-knobbed sawback *(Graptemys nigrinoda pelticola)* is found mostly in Alabama and Mississippi. *Above, bottom:* The ringed sawback lives only in the Pearl River of southern Mississippi and adjacent Louisiana. *Above, right:* The Mississippi map turtle *(Graptemys kohni)* can always be identified by its distinctive white iris and the light crescent behind each eye. *Right:* The Sabine map turtle *(Graptemys pseudogeographica sabinensis)* is a subspecies of the false map turtle. It is found in the Sabine River, which separates Louisiana from Texas. *Far right:* The Barbour's map turtle *(Graptemys barbour)* exhibits extreme sexual dimorphism: Females are sometimes more than twice as large as males.

© Dr. E.R. Degginger

Above: Ornate diamondback terrapins *(Malaclemys macrospilota)* are identified by the orange-yellow centers of the carapacial scutes. Along with green turtle soup, the use of diamondback terrapins as a luxury food item is perhaps the most celebrated example of turtle cuisine. From the late 1800s until about 1920, terrapin meat was a much-sought-after commodity, and many terrapins were raised commercially.

Terrapins

Closely related to map turtles, diamondback terrapins (genus *Malaclemys*) consist of one species (*Malaclemys terrapin*) and seven subspecies, found exclusively in coastal waters and brackish marshes, estuaries, and lagoons from Massachusetts all the way to the Gulf coast of southeast Texas.

Diamondback terrapins are medium-sized turtles (5 to 10 inches [13 to 25 centimeters] long); the head is thick and blunt, and the head and legs are covered with spots instead of stripes. Most species have strongly inscribed, concentric rings on the carapace plates; these are raised in the center, accounting for the name "diamondback." They have large, webbed rear feet.

As with map turtles, female diamondbacks are nearly twice as large as males and have larger heads. Diamondbacks are primarily carnivorous, and some of their food is obtained by scavenging. They hibernate in winter, though they may emerge for warm periods. They are most active during the day and sleep buried in the mud at night.

Diamondbacks are perhaps best known for their popularity as a gourmet food item during the late nineteenth century and in the 1920s. In fact, large "farms" were established (notably at Beaufort, North Carolina) to raise them; ironically, this measure undoubtedly saved some populations from decimation and perhaps extinction.

Archie Carr characterized the diamondback's popularity as a delicacy as largely a fad "as synthetic as the latest Paris fashion. I don't mean to say that diamondbacks aren't good eating," he said. "I merely suggest that the difference between a seven-dollar diamondback and a forty-cent soft-shell of the same weight is to a considerable degree a difference in the state of mind of the consumer."

©A.B. Sheldon

© David M. Dennis/Tom Stack & Associates

Above: The head of a northern diamondback terrapin, found from Cape Cod south to Cape Hatteras, North Carolina. *Left:* This variety of Caspian turtle, *Mauremys caspica caspica,* lives in western Iran, Iraq, and parts of Turkey.

POND AND BOX TURTLES

Pond Turtles

In North America, there are four species of pond turtles (genus *Clemmys*), popularly known as the spotted turtle, the wood turtle, the bog turtle (or Muhlenberg's turtle), and the Western pond turtle. The first three, which are found only in the northeastern United States and adjoining parts of Canada, are equally aquatic and terrestrial, while the Western pond turtle (which lives on the West Coast of North America, from the state of Washington south into Baja California) rarely leaves the water except to bask.

Generally, pond turtles are medium-sized (5 to 9 inches [13 to 23 centimeters] in carapace length). The bog turtle, however, is an exception; at slightly more than 4 inches (10 centimeters), it may be the smallest species of turtle in the world. All species are omnivorous, eating worms, snails, insects, crayfish, carrion, as well as fruits and grasses. The Western pond turtle is the most carnivorous.

Male and female pond turtles are about the same size, and with the exception that males usually have a concave plastron, the sexes are not dramatically different in appearance. Females lay from three to twelve eggs in shallow nests, which they frequently take great care to camouflage.

The spotted turtle (*Clemmys guttata*) has a smooth, bluish black carapace with yellow spots. Juveniles have very few spots, and more appear as the animal gets older. The spots may fade on very old specimens. The skin is gray to black and is occasionally spotted, too.

Spotted turtles are small (4 to 5 inches [10 to 13 centimeters]), mild-mannered, and shy; they burrow in the mud when disturbed in the water and retreat into their shells when threatened on land. Compared with most emydid turtles, they prefer cold temperatures, though they hibernate underwater in the coldest parts of winter. Spotted turtles have recorded lifespans of more than forty years.

Above, top: The spotted turtle *(Clemys guttata)* and wood turtle *(Clemys insculpta [above, bottom])* are emydids that live in the eastern and northeastern United States. The latter is hardy and intelligent, making it a suitable pet, though it is protected over much of its range.

© A.B. Sheldon

The wood turtle (*Clemmys insculpta*) is larger than the spotted turtle, averaging about 7 inches (18 centimeters) in length. Striking in appearance, it has a rough, keeled shell that flares at the edges; a flat, frequently jet-black head; orange limbs and throat; and a long tail. As the name implies, wood turtles are mainly terrestrial, frequenting bodies of water only at times of mating or hibernation.

Wood turtles are most active during the day, when they wander about in woods and meadows. Their range appears to be limited; individuals who have been captured and released frequently are recaptured, even years later, very close to where they were originally found. Wood turtles are accomplished climbers—they have been seen ascending chainlink fences. The oldest wood turtle on record lived fifty-eight years.

Many authorities comment on the superior intelligence of the wood turtle. Archie Carr cites some experiments with mazes in which it was "decided that its ability to learn new routes was about equal to that of a rat, which, though it has an uncomplimentary ring, is really pretty good for a turtle; and anyway, in a personality contest a wood turtle would win from a rat in a walk."

Because of its intelligence and genial, extroverted nature, wood turtles are prized as pets by many turtle collectors. Carr kept one in the house for eighteen months: "She slept in a closet and showed up at the breakfast table every morning where she made for my wife's chair, craned her neck expectantly, and often stood on three legs with one foot lifted and poised like a pointer dog that smells birds."

Bog turtles (*Clemmys muhlenbergi*) have,

The bog turtle *(Clemys insculpta)*, or Muhlenberg's turtle, is perhaps the smallest species of turtle in the world, rarely exceeding 4 inches (10 cm) in length.

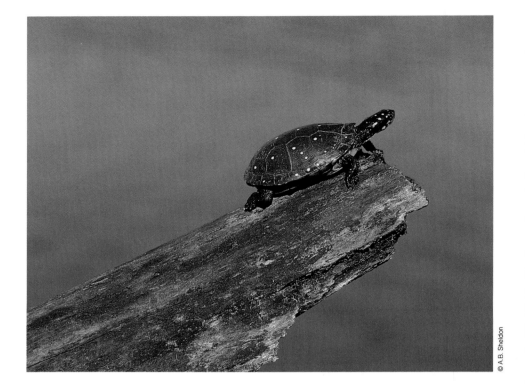

Spotted turtles *(Clemys guttata)* are fairly small animals, rarely exceeding 5 inches (13 cm) in carapace length.

according to Pritchard, "perhaps the most rigid habitat preferences of any North American freshwater turtle. It is usually found in sphagnum bogs, in situations where it can walk about in very shallow water."

The bog turtle is of interest for its small size and discontinuous range (it is found in parts of New York, New Jersey, Massachusetts, Connecticut, Pennsylvania, and Maryland). Human beings are rapidly encroaching on the bog turtle's territory, and it is a threatened species.

The range of pond turtles in North America extends only as far west as Wisconsin, and then, oddly, it picks up again on the West Coast with the Pacific pond turtle (*Clemmys marmorata*). Medium-sized (about 6 inches [15 centimeters]) and olive to black in color, it is thoroughly aquatic except when basking or digging a nest. Shy and wary, it plunges into the water at the least disturbance.

Box Turtles

Four species of box turtles (genus *Terrapene*) inhabit North America: Two are abundant and widespread in the United States, while smaller populations of all four species are found in Mexico.

Box turtles, which are largely terrestrial, are medium-sized turtles (6 to 8 inches [15 to 20 centimeters] long) with several distinctive physical features: a colorful, ornate,

domed shell that is longer than it is wide; a plastral hinge that allows them to withdraw completely into their shells; and large rear feet, which are neither webbed (and therefore unsuited for swimming) nor elephantine (like the feet of the tortoises that box turtles resemble). Additionally, the upper jaws of box turtles have a slight hook at the tip, and the rear feet have prominent claws. Male box turtles have bright red eyes; the female's are light brown.

Box turtles are strictly diurnal; after dark, they burrow or find some place to conceal themselves for the night. Their home range is limited (a radius of several hundred yards is typical). Box turtles are omnivorous, eating fruit, carrion, vegetation, insects, small vertebrates, and worms.

Nesting takes place from May through July; clutch sizes range from two to eight eggs. Nests are destroyed by skunks, foxes, raccoons, and crows. Snakes, crows, coyotes, foxes, dogs, and skunks eat juveniles. Man is the greatest destroyer of adult box turtles—thousands are crushed on the highway every year. Because it is hardy, even-tempered, adaptable, and long-lived, the box turtle, like the wood turtle, is a favored pet among turtle fanciers.

The eastern box turtle (*Terrapene carolina*) is found primarily in the open woods of almost every state south of the Great Lakes and east of the Mississippi River, plus Kansas, Missouri, Oklahoma, Arkansas, Louisiana, eastern Texas, and the Mexican states of Campeche, Quintana Roo, San Luis Potosi, Tamaulipas, Veracruz, and Yucatan.

Usually, the eastern box turtle has a brown or black carapace decorated with red or yellow stripes, dots, or smudges, often in a pattern that looks like it might have been painted by a small child.

The western (or "ornate") box turtle (*Terrapene ornata*) inhabits the treeless plains, prairies, and rolling country covered with grass and scattered low brush in the southwestern, central, and south-central United States and western Mexico. It is smaller than the eastern box turtle, the maximum length being about 6 inches (15 centimeters). The decorative pattern on the western box turtle's shell is somewhat different, too: It has a dark brown or black carapace with yellow lines radiating outward from the center of each scute.

CHICKEN AND BLANDING'S TURTLES

The remaining emydid turtles in the United States consist of two genera of one species each, Blanding's turtle (*Emydoidea blandingi*) and the chicken turtle (*Deirochelys reticularia*). Both are medium-sized turtles (maximum size: about 10 inches [25 centimeters]) with long necks and narrow jaw surfaces; both prefer still waters, such as ponds, swamps, and drainage ditches.

The Blanding's turtle lives in the north-central United States—near the Great Lakes and slightly to the west—and just north, in southern Canada. It has a smooth, dark carapace covered with yellow speckles and resembles a European pond turtle, to which it was once thought to be closely related. It has several other distinguishing features; prominent eyes, a long neck, a plastral hinge, and a yellow throat and lower jaw. Blanding's turtles, which are completely aquatic except for when they bask, are omnivorous but show a preference for crayfish.

The chicken turtle (named for the taste of its flesh) is found in the southern and south-central United States. It has a medium-brown, slightly sculpted shell, a striped neck two-thirds the length of its carapace, and distinctive vertical stripes on its thighs. It is omnivorous but prefers small invertebrates. Unlike Blanding's turtle, the chicken turtle spends a good deal of time wandering on land.

OTHER NEW WORLD EMYDIDS

One other genus of emydid turtles is found in the Western Hemisphere. Known as *Rhinoclemys,* it consists of nine species of terrestrial and semiterrestrial turtles that range from southern Sonora, in western Mexico, southward through Central America, and into Ecuador and northern Brazil in South America.

These turtles resemble box turtles, but they are larger and lack a plastral hinge. All have been fully described by herpetologists,

© Dr. E.R. Degginger

The Florida box turtle *(Terrapene carolina bauri)* resides in southern Georgia and throughout Florida.

© A.B. Sheldon

Above: Blanding's turtle *(Emydoidea blandingi),* a medium-sized, carnivorous North American emydid. *Right:* A closeup of a box turtle. Interestingly, box turtle meat is frequently poisonous to humans because of residue from poisonous fungi that make up part of the turtle's diet.

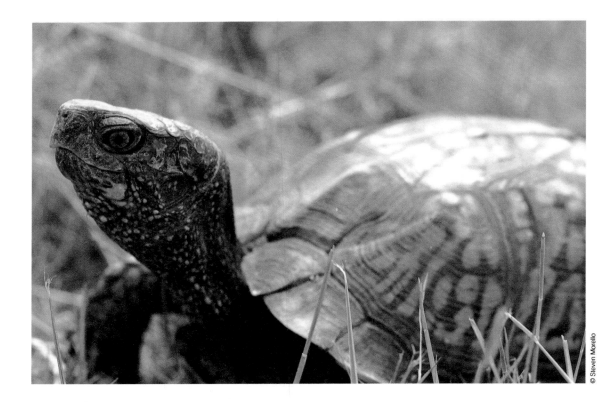

© Steven Morello

but little is known about the habits of many members of this genus, so only the most significant and/or unusual will be included here.

One widespread species is known popularly as the Mexican red turtle or Mexican wood turtle (*Rhinoclemys pulcherrima*), which lives in Mexico and Central America and is distinguished by thin red and black wormlike lines on its face, limbs, and tail. This is an omnivorous, fundamentally terrestrial turtle that grows to a typical carapace length of about 6 inches (15 centimeters). The largest and most aquatic member of the genus is *Rhinoclemys funera*, which is found in eastern Central America. It has a black carapace and grows to a maximum length of 13 inches (33 centimeters).

South American varieties of *Rhinoclemys* are unusual in that females usually lay a single, large egg (3 inches by 1½ inches [8 centimeters by 4 centimeters]) that is sometimes nearly half the length of the turtle itself. In tropical climates, several eggs can be laid each year, and the larger hatchlings have a better chance to survive.

EUROPEAN EMYDIDS

The principal difference between the way emydid turtles are distributed in the Americas and in Europe is that in the Americas there are relatively few genera but many species, while in Europe, there are many genera but few species; in fact, many genera consist of but a single species.

Only three species of emydid turtles live in areas surrounding the Mediterranean Sea. One of the best known is the European pond turtle (*Emys orbicularis*), which resembles Blanding's turtle, having a black carapace with light yellow speckles. It is found in Spain, central France, northern Italy, southern Germany, Poland, northern Turkey and Iran, northern Morocco, Algeria, and Tunisia. This small (5 to 6 inch [13 to 15 centimeters]), carnivorous turtle has been popular as a pet among British turtle fanciers, though the weather in England is too cold for pond turtles that live outdoors to breed.

Another Mediterranean emydid is the Spanish turtle (*Mauremys leprosa*), which lives in Spain, Portugal, Morocco, Algeria, Libya, and Tunisia. An aquatic, carnivorous species, the Spanish turtle often lives in filthy mudholes and becomes infested with parasites and covered with algae; hence, its Latin name.

A close relative, the Caspian turtle (*Mauremys caspica*), lives in the Middle East (Iran, Iraq, Turkey, Syria, and Israel) as well as parts of Greece, Crete, and Yugoslavia. The male Caspian turtle is reputed to be extremely violent toward the female during mating, biting her neck with such viciousness that the wounds often prove fatal. Two relatives of the Caspian turtle, *Mauremys mutica* and *Mauremys japonica,* live in China and southern Japan, respectively.

ASIAN EMYDIDS

The rest of the world's emydid turtles, some thirty-plus genera, live in Asia—principally in India, Bangladesh, China, Taiwan, and mainland Southeast Asia (including Burma, Thailand, Vietnam, and Malaysia).

Little is known of the behavior of many of these asiatic turtles, so again only the most significant and unusual are described here.

The Brahminy river turtle (*Hardella thurji*) lives in the Ganges, Brahmaputra, and Indus river systems in India. A large turtle (females grow to 21 inches [53 centi-

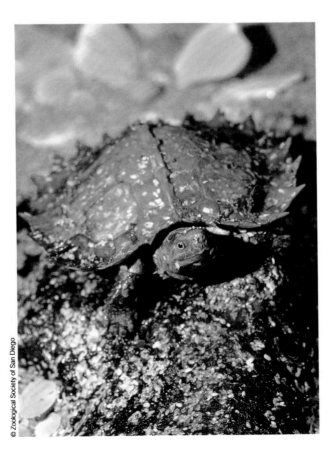

The serrated turtle, a large east African sideneck, often reaches a length of more than 15 inches (38 cm) and a weight of more than 20 pounds (8 kg).

meters]), it is an important food source, and great numbers are sold in Calcutta. The size differences between males and females are greater in this species than in any other known species; males grow to a reported maximum length of just 7 inches (18 centimeters). The Brahminy river turtle is herbivorous and is reported to have a gentle disposition. Its carapace is dark brown or black.

Another large aquatic species is the common batagur or tuntong (*Batagur baska*), found in the rivers of Sumatra, Thailand, Burma, and the Malay Peninsula. It grows to a length of about 2 feet (61 centimeters), and females lay clutches of ten to thirty eggs, 3 inches (8 centimeters) long, which are collected by the humans in the countries where they are found.

The turtle gets the second of its popular names from the drumming sound a nesting female makes—"tun tonk"—when she drops herself on the sand to compact her nest after laying the eggs and covering them. Sometimes natives can hear hundreds of batagurs nesting simultaneously.

The biuku turtle (*Callagur borneoensis*), found in Borneo, Sumatra, and the Malay Peninsula, may be the largest of all emydid turtles, reaching a carapace length of 30 inches (76 centimeters). Its distinctive features are a covering of skin (instead of scales) on top of its head and a gray-brown carapace with three black, longitudinal bands.

The spiny turtle (*Heosemys spinosa*), an emydid from Southeast Asia that grows to 8 or 9 inches (20 or 23 centimeters) long, looks like a cogwheel; it has a raised, spiny keel and marginals (scutes around the edge of the carapace).

Three of the five Asiatic box turtles (genus *Cuora*), like their American counterparts (*Terrapene*), have well-developed plastral hinges, which allow them to shut their soft parts completely within the protective surrounding of their shells. One of the more abundant species is the Malayan box turtle (*Cuora amboinensis*), an herbivorous species that is mostly aquatic, inhabiting ponds, marshes, and flooded rice paddies.

A turtle common to southern China that has also been introduced to other parts of the world (including the United States) is Reeves' turtle (*Chinemys reevesi*). It grows to slightly more than 12 inches (31 centimeters) in length and has brown carapace scutes edged in yellow or white. An omnivorous turtle that is hardy in captivity, Reeves' turtle is popular as a pet.

Reeves' turtle *(Chinemys reevesi)*, an Asian emydid, possesses a hardy constitution, and as such is popular as a pet.

TORTOISES

Next to emydid turtles, tortoises (family Testudinidae) make up the largest category of the world's chelonians: There are ten genera and about thirty-nine species worldwide, the greatest diversity of which are found in Africa.

Tortoises are the only turtles—except for a few emydids—completely adapted for life on land. They differ from other types of turtles in several ways: they have hard, horny shells with distinct, well-defined growth rings (annuli) on each lamina; front feet that are slightly flattened from front to back, with thick scales on the front; stumplike, elephantine rear legs; a mostly herbivorous diet; and an almost exclusively terrestrial habitat. Tortoises are generally considered to have evolved from emydid turtles.

It is not possible to talk about tortoises without bringing human beings into the discussion in a significant way, because, beginning about 400 years ago, mankind has had a crucial, devastating, and irreversible influence on the very existence of many species of tortoises—millions were slaughtered, and nearly a dozen species (all of the genus *Geochelone*) are now considered "recently extinct" or "almost extinct." In some ways, the manner in which people treated tortoises in the seventeenth and eighteenth centuries parallels the way many species of sea turtles have been treated in modern times.

The largest and most widely distributed genus of tortoises is *Geochelone*; sixteen species are found throughout Africa, Southeast Asia, Madagascar, Celebes (an island in Indonesia), Aldabra (an island in the Indian Ocean), and the Galapagos Islands (east of Ecuador). All larger tortoises belong to this genus; the most famous are the gigantic species inhabiting the Galapagos Islands and those, similar in appearance but descended from different ancestors, now living almost half a world away on the island of Aldabra.

A Galapagos tortoise (*Geochelone elephantopus*) may reach a carapace length of 4 feet (1.2 m) and a weight of 500 pounds (187 kg). Its legs are extremely strong and are capable of bearing a man's weight on its back.

GALAPAGOS TORTOISES

The Galapagos Islands lie about 600 miles (960 kilometers) east of Ecuador, on the equator. Comprised of a group of about twenty volcanic islands, the Galapagos archipelago was discovered by Spanish sailors in 1535. Giant tortoises (*Geochelone elephantopus*) lived on eleven of these islands in incredibly abundant numbers. In many places, it has been written, the islands were so densely populated with tortoises that a person could walk on their backs for long distances without ever setting foot on the ground beneath them.

Originally, there were about fourteen different subspecies of tortoises living on the Galapagos, separated from each other by the ocean or impassable stretches of fresh lava. Galapagos tortoises reach a maximum carapace length of nearly 4 feet (1.2 meters) and may weigh 500 pounds (187 kilograms) or more. The shape of the carapace varies depending on the subspecies—some are domed, some are flatter, some are distinctly "saddlebacked" (elevated above the neck). The color of the carapace is dark brown, dark green, or black. Head and neck size also vary according to subspecies, though most have long necks, which allows them to reach plants that grow several feet off the ground, such as certain varieties of cactus. With their large, powerful legs, the giant tortoises are able to scramble over rocky ground.

Male Galapagos tortoises are much larger than females; their size advantage helps them in courtship rituals, which are abbreviated and direct: Males simply overpower females, battering them with the front of their shells and immobilizing them with their weight. Females nest throughout the year, choosing a place that receives direct sunlight. A clutch of ten eggs is typical. Both males and females mature slowly, taking about twenty to twenty-five years.

Galapagos tortoises spend much of their time wallowing in the mud near water holes and swamps. Depending on the ambient temperature, they may partially submerge themselves in ponds. At night, many burrow in soft ground or vegetation. In dry weather, Galapagos tortoises migrate to the moist highlands, moving back to the lowlands during periods of rainy weather. They will eat al-

© Ann Reilly/Photo/Nats

most any green vegetation they can find.

These tortoises lived relatively undisturbed until the nineteenth century, when hunters in search of seals and whales landed on the islands. Galapagos tortoises became a readily available source of meat for these men. At first, whalers simply brought large numbers of the mild-mannered tortoises on board ship where, left virtually unattended and uncared for, they were killed as needed.

Later, when whales became scarce, the hunters discovered that oil could be obtained from the fat and eggs of tortoises. According to whalers' logs, some 200,000 were slaughtered, often wastefully, within a thirty-year period, and it has been estimated that more than 10 million have been killed since the discovery of the Galapagos Islands nearly 500 years ago. Tortoises also perished as a result of the cultivation of the land and consequent destruction of their habitats, and through the introduction of feral mammals such as dogs, goats, pigs, and rats, which compete for food, destroy nests, and kill juveniles.

In this century, conservation and breeding programs have been undertaken, and al-

Over the centuries, hundreds of thousands, possibly millions, of Galapagos tortoises have been slaughtered by human beings.

though several subspecies have become extinct or endangered, there are perhaps 10,000 tortoises remaining in the Galapagos today, and they are not considered critically endangered.

In 1964, two significant steps were taken to ensure the tortoises' well-being: The Darwin Memorial Research Station was founded on one of the islands, and the archipelago was established as a national park of Ecuador, further protecting the tortoise. One of the most important tasks that has been undertaken to preserve the tortoise is the destruction of the wild animals with which they cannot successfully compete.

Less well known but equally tragic was the fate of the subspecies of giant tortoises living on islands in the Indian Ocean, which were very similar in appearance to those on the Galapagos Islands.

In the sixteenth century, travellers rounding the Cape of Good Hope heading toward India discovered a number of islands inhabited by unusual animals. In 1598, the first Dutch sailors reached Mauritius, a small island east of Madagascar. Here they found large, trusting, flightless birds and giant tortoises, both of whom they slaughtered in huge numbers.

It only took a few years for the birds—dodos—to become extinct, and by the mid-1700s, the number of tortoises on Mauritius had been drastically reduced. They were found to be living on nearby smaller islands, and were imported to Mauritius to be sold to passing naval, merchant, or pirate ships. Gradually, island by island, the giant tortoises on Diego Rodriguez, Reunion, Mauritius, Farquhar, and the Seychelles Archipelago were almost completely exterminated.

By the end of the nineteenth century the only significant numbers of giant tortoises were those living on the island of Aldabra. They survived only because the island is off the direct sea route to India.

To prevent the destruction of all the giants, a number of famous British naturalists—Charles Darwin among them—initiated protective measures, mainly exportation and captive breeding. Tortoises from Aldabra were taken to Mauritius, and breeding farms were established. Today, about 100,000 tortoises live in the wild and on Aldabra; tortoises are also found in lesser numbers on Mauritius and Zanzibar.

Giant tortoises have the potential to live very long lives. Several are on record as having lived more than 100 years. Perhaps the oldest, known as "Marion's tortoise" of Mauritius, lived for 152 years before an accident ended its life in 1918.

Because of their great size and, therefore, their economic value, the giant tortoises of the Galapagos and the islands off Madagascar are unique in the extent to which they have been exploited by human beings.

Right: Steps have been taken by the government of Ecuador and private organizations to preserve the Galapagos tortoise. *Opposite page:* Originally, there were fourteen distinct populations of giant tortoises on the Galapagos Islands before man began to kill them in large numbers in the nineteenth century.

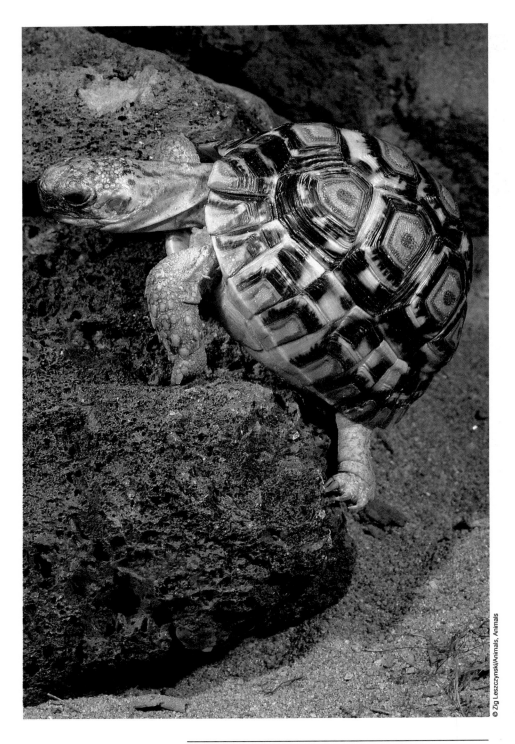

The leopard tortoise, a large African species with distinctive markings and a domed carapace.

OTHER TORTOISES FROM AFRICA AND MADAGASCAR

Other significant African tortoises of the genus *Geochelone* include the spurred tortoise and the leopard tortoise. The spurred tortoise (*Geochelone sulcata*), found across the broadest section of north-central Africa, is the largest mainland tortoise, growing to more than 30 inches (76 centimeters) and 200 pounds (75 kilograms). Males are much bigger than females.

The carapace of the spurred tortoise is a uniform yellow or bone color; the laminae and growth rings are generally well defined. The spurred tortoise is named for two or three strong spines, or spurs, on each side of its tail. Because it lives in arid desert regions, the spurred tortoise may have to go without water for years at a time. A thick, highly impermeable skin, plus its habit of digging deep burrows in hot weather, prevent moisture loss.

The leopard tortoise (*Geochelone pardalis*) is smaller (2 feet [60 centimeters] long, 70 pounds [26 kilograms]) than the spurred tortoise; its range extends over the plains of most of central and southern Africa, where there is more vegetation available than in the range of the spurred tortoise. A hardy species, the leopard tortoise makes a good pet. Not surprisingly, it is named for its domed, decorative carapace—black spots and blotches on a yellow background.

Each of the laminae of the radiated tortoise of Madagascar (*Geochelone radiata*) are slightly conical, with a black-on-yellow star pattern radiating from the center. Males and females grow to about 15 inches (38 centimeters) and a weight of 28 pounds (10 kilograms). Radiated tortoises are protected by law and venerated by natives, who will not harm them. Unfortunately, many Chinese in Madagascar will pay a high price for the turtle, because they consider its flesh to be an aphrodisiac. The starred tortoise of India (*Geochelone elegans*) is very similar to the radiated tortoise, but smaller (females grow to 10 inches [25 centimeters]; males to 6 inches [15 centimeters]).

One of the most famous and long-lived of all turtles was a radiated tortoise, "Tui Malila," reputedly presented to the Queen of Tonga by Captain Cook in 1773 or 1777. It lived until May 19, 1966—and survived at least one forest fire as well as a severe kick by a horse. At the end of its life, it was completely blind and had to be fed by hand.

One of the most interesting African tortoises is the pancake tortoise (*Malacochersus tornieri*), which lives in Kenya and Tanzania. Unlike other tortoises, which have hard, domed shells, the pancake tortoise has a flat, soft shell. Pancake tortoises reach a length of about 6 inches (15 centimeters); the carapace is usually pale brown with dark brown or black borders to the laminae. The pancake tortoise eats vegetation; females lay a single egg.

Pancake tortoises are capable of climbing rocks and can typically be found under them. When molested, instead of withdrawing into its shell, the pancake tortoise runs and wedges itself into a rocky crevice. There, it inflates its lungs, rendering itself nearly immovable.

The hinge-back tortoise (*Kinixys erosa*), which lives across most of central Africa just north of the equator, is unique in that it is the only tortoise with a hinged carapace, consisting of cartilaginous material located at the junction of the second and third costal (side) laminae, or about in the middle of the shell. This gives the tortoise the ability to completely tuck in its hind feet and tail when threatened. Hingeback tortoises have brown carapaces and yellow heads; they grow to a maximum length of about 13 inches (33 centimeters).

EUROPEAN TORTOISES

Five species of tortoises, all of the genus *Testudo*, are found in Europe and areas surrounding the Mediterranean Sea. One of the best-known is the Mediterranean spur-thigh tortoise (*Testudo graeca*), which lives in North Africa, the Near East, and extreme southern Europe. It has a moderately domed carapace 7 to 8 inches (18 to 20 centimeters) in length, of a dull yellow or olive color. The anterior portion of each lamina has a black border, and each thigh has a prominent spur. The spur-thigh tortoise hibernates in cold weather; females normally lay only two or three eggs per clutch.

This tortoise has been the most popular pet tortoise in Britain; at one time, 300,000 per year were shipped from Morocco to

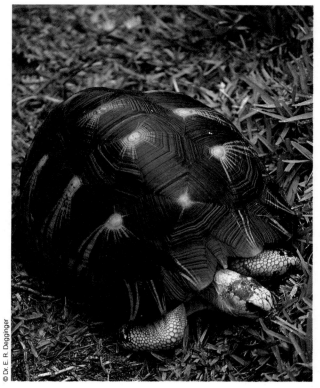

Top: The African pancake tortoise, which wedges itself between rocks to escape danger. *Bottom:* The radiated tortoise of Madagascar. Its meat is believed by some natives to have aphrodisiac properties.

Above, top: The Chilean or Chaco tortoise *(Geochelone chilensis),* a South American species taken as a pet and also used for food. *Above, bottom:* The Indian star tortoise *(Testudo radiata),* an exotic species closely related to the leopard tortoise.

England. Unfortunately, upward of 90 percent died within a year, because the British climate was too cold and damp for them. Under appropriate conditions, this tortoise can live to be very old—some have lived for more than 100 years.

Hermann's tortoise (*Testudo hermanni*) is found only in Europe (southern Italy, Sicily, Yugoslavia, Albania, Bulgaria, Turkey, and Rumania). It is very similar in appearance to *Testudo graeca,* except that it lacks thigh spurs and is smaller. Hermann's tortoise, which has a sharp spine on the tip of its tail, is also popular as a pet turtle.

The largest member of the genus is the margined tortoise (*Testudo marginata*), which is found only in southern Greece. It grows to 12 inches (30 centimeters) in length, with an elongated shell and flared marginals at the back of the carapace of males.

ASIAN TORTOISES

Seven species of tortoises, all genus *Geochelone,* live in India, Celebes, and Southeast Asia; one (the starred tortoise of India, *Geochelone elegans*), has been mentioned. Another, the Burmese brown tortoise (*Geochelone emys*) is considered one of the two most primitive living tortoises (that is, resembling emydids, from which tortoises are derived) because of its flattened shell and preference for living in moist, tropical forests, among other qualities. The Burmese brown tortoise is the largest of the Asian tortoises (with a maximum carapace length of 18 inches [46 centimeters]) and lives in Burma, Thailand, the Malay Peninsula, Sumatra, and Borneo. It is prized as a food source throughout its range.

SOUTH AMERICAN TORTOISES

In mainland South America, there are three species of tortoises, again all genus *Geochelone,* which are very abundant and range over virtually the entire continent: the yellow-footed tortoise (*Geochelone denticulata*), the red-footed tortoise (*Geochelone carbonaria*), and the Chaco or Argentine tortoise (*Geochelone chilensis*).

© Gerry Ellis/Ellis Wildlife Collection

The yellow-footed tortoise, sometimes known as the Hercules, jaboty, or Brazilian giant tortoise, is found in the dense rain forests and tropical lowlands of South America. Sexual differences are pronounced in this species: Females grow to a length of 2 or 2½ feet (60 to 76 centimeters), while males rarely exceed 16 inches (40 centimeters). The shape of the carapace is different, too: Males have long, low shells with a deeply concave plastron; females have high, narrow shells with a flat plastron.

In mature turtles of both sexes, the shell is thick and heavy—dark brown with patches of yellow on each scute. The plastron is also dark brown, and the limbs and head are brown with some orange scales and markings.

Yellow-footed tortoises live hidden in the thick forest undergrowth (avoiding clearings and wide trails); they prefer a diet of leaves

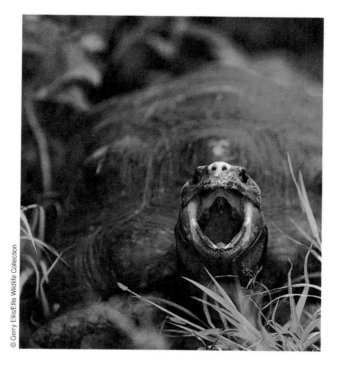

© Gerry Ellis/Ellis Wildlife Collection

Above and left: The red-footed tortoise *(Geochelone carbonaria)* is a strikingly marked, medium-sized turtle found throughout South America.

and fruit, though they occasionally eat insects and will eat meat in captivity. They are highly valued as food; Pritchard reports that natives often set whole hillsides afire, then "walk through afterward and pick up the exposed (and presumably roasted) tortoises."

The closely related red-footed tortoise, which inhabits roughly the same areas as *Geochelone denticulata,* is smaller than the yellow-footed, reaching a length of about 17 inches (43 centimeters), the males being a little larger than females. The carapace is black with an indentation in the center, giving it a slightly hourglass shape when looked at from above, and there are red and reddish yellow scales on the legs and head, which are also black. Each of the laminae has some red or reddish yellow marking, too. The red-footed tortoise is found in open prairies as well as in forests.

The two above-mentioned tortoises engage in interesting courtship behavior. If a male yellow-footed encounters another yellow-footed, it walks to the side of it and then moves its head suddenly sideways, usually toward the tortoise, then quickly back to the center position. If the other tortoise is a male, it will respond similarly. If not, the first tortoise will walk to the back of the other and sniff its cloacal region to verify that it is a female. If that's the case, the male initiates copulation almost immediately. The red-footed tortoise makes slightly different head movements and emits a henlike "clucking" sound when copulating.

The range of the Chaco tortoise extends further south than that of the others; it is abundant in Argentina and Chile, sometimes reaching a population density of fifteen to twenty per acre. It grows to about 14 inches (35 centimeters) in length, and females are slightly larger than males. The carapace is yellow-brown with darker laminar edges, which is useful for camouflage. The Chaco tortoise is also used for food and is considered an endangered species by some authorities.

NORTH AMERICAN TORTOISES

All four North American tortoises belong to the genus *Gopherus*: the gopher tortoise, the desert tortoise, the Texas tortoise, and the Bolson tortoise.

The gopher tortoise (*Gopherus polyphemus*) is distributed over the largest geographical area—Florida, southern Mississippi, Alabama, the southern half of Georgia, and extreme eastern Louisiana—though none of the four tortoises lives in a particularly large area, and no species' territory overlaps another's.

The gopher tortoise usually grows to slightly less than a foot in length (the record is about 16 inches [40 centimeters]) and a weight of 29 pounds (11 kilograms). Its carapace is brown with well-defined annular rings, and the plastron is yellow. Also, the hind feet are comparatively small.

"Gophers" have two distinct physical characteristics: The gular laminae (the foremost laminae of the plastron) normally extend quite far forward under the neck and chin of the tortoise (males use them as battering rams), and their forelimbs are flattened, with rigid wrists.

The latter feature gives the gopher tortoise the ability to engage in the activity from which it derives its name: to dig long burrows that become its home at night and during periods of cold weather.

Gophers often live in the transitional zones between two ecosystems, such as woodland and pasture. They begin burrow-

The South American yellow-footed tortoise (*Geochelone denticulata*), known as "jaboty" in Brazil. A vegetarian, this tortoise lives in dense rain forests and is prized as a food source by humans.

© Zoological Society of San Diego

ing, typically in loose or sandy soil, from the time they are hatchlings; they are quite territorial, and a tortoise may inhabit a single burrow for most of its life, never roaming far from it. Burrows may be as long as 30 feet (9 meters) and as deep as 12 feet (3.6 meters); they may be straight or curved and may have an enlarged chamber in them. Gopher tortoises are active year round and only hibernate briefly during very cold periods.

A burrow provides the tortoise with an easy escape from the hot sun; the temperature in the burrow is more constant and the humidity greater. Normally, gopher tortoises emerge from their burrows when the day begins to get warm. They feed on nearby leaves and grasses, sometimes along well-defined "grazing trails." Usually, they return in the early afternoon. If disturbed or frightened near its burrow, a gopher tortoise will head rapidly toward it and wedge itself inside by extending its feet and head.

Other animals frequently share the burrows of gopher tortoises. These include beetles, cave crickets, spiders, lizards, gopher frogs, gopher mice, and an occasional snake. None of these cause the gopher tortoise any benefit or harm, though sometimes tortoises die when humans, trying to flush out rattlesnakes, pour gasoline down gopher holes and set them afire.

When courting, male gopher tortoises walk in a circle around females, bobbing their heads up and down to attract them; for some reason, this seems to work. Next, males bite females on the legs and on the front edge of their shells to encourage submissiveness and immobility, upon which mating commences. Females make nests from April through July, normally laying four to seven eggs.

Though skunks, raccoons, and snakes destroy nests and eat hatchlings, human beings are the principal killer of adult gopher tortoises: encroaching upon their territory with housing developments, agriculture, and shopping centers; running over tortoises on the road; and, before the gopher tortoise was protected, capturing adults and juveniles for use as pets, where they do poorly and rarely survive.

The desert tortoise (*Gopherus agassizi*) lives in southern Nevada, southeastern California, western Arizona, and extreme south-

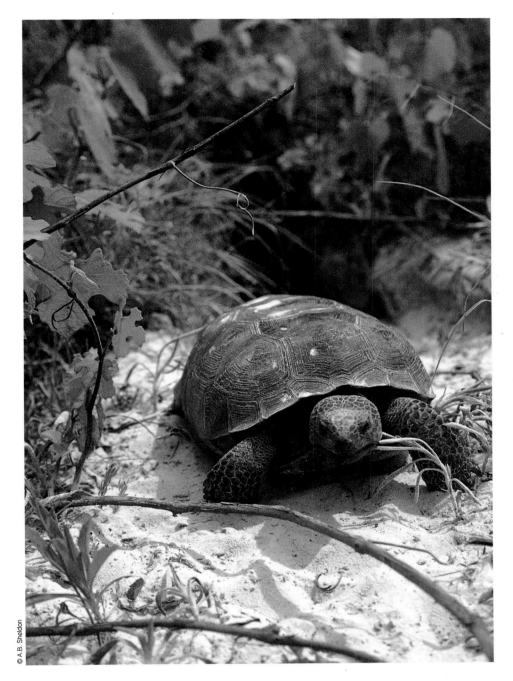

© A.B. Sheldon

western Utah in the United States, plus northern Baja California, western Sonora, and northwestern Sinaloa in Mexico. It is about the same size and color as the gopher tortoise, with prominent growth rings on the carapace and elongated gular laminae. Sometimes there are yellow or orange patches in the center of each lamina. Its hind feet are larger than those of the gopher tortoise, however, and its head is narrower.

The habitat of the desert tortoise is more severe than that of the gopher tortoise— temperatures are both hotter and colder, the humidity is lower and there is less water available—so it must live its life differently.

In northern regions, the desert tortoise has both a "summer" and a "winter" range. In summer, because it tolerates heat well, the desert tortoise wanders over arid, flat desert

The Florida gopher tortoise (*Gopherus polyphemus*) is a distant relative of the desert tortoise.

and dry stream beds, retiring at night to shallow burrows (2 to 4 feet [60 centimeters to 1.2 meters] deep) it digs in gravelly or sandy soil near the base of shrubs. In winter, in order to survive periods of extreme cold, it hibernates in the foothills (sometimes communally) in larger, deeper burrows (15 feet [4.5 meters] long or more, dug in hard ground). At the southern extremes of its range, it has no need to burrow at all.

The desert tortoise is herbivorous, eating grasses, leaves, cactus pads, and desert flowers. Usually, it forages actively in the early morning and late afternoon. Because it lives in such dry climates, the desert tortoise is capable of going for a year or more without drinking water. It is also able to store and reabsorb water from its bladder, excreting nitrogenous wastes in the form of semi-solid urates instead of urinating.

The mating habits of the desert tortoise are similar to those of the gopher tortoise. Male desert tortoises are aggressive toward one another, frequently fighting, especially during mating season (spring and early summer). The desert tortoise reaches sexual maturity slowly (fifteen to twenty years).

As is the case with the gopher tortoise, the desert tortoise makes a poor pet, requiring specialized care. Desert tortoises are protected in the United States as an endangered species by the U.S. Fish and Wildlife Service. Still, many are run over on the roads and deserts by cars and off-road vehicles, many are still taken as pets, many must compete (unsuccessfully) with cattle for food, and many are cruelly used for target practice.

The Texas tortoise (*Gopherus berlandieri*) is the smallest of the four species found in North America; it grows to a length of only 6 or 7 inches (15 or 18 centimeters). It lives in the southern one-third of Texas, plus the Mexican states of Coahuila, Nuevo León, and Tamaulipas.

It has a rounded, brown shell with yellow patches and extended, forked gular laminae. As the Texas tortoise ages, its shell lightens to a uniform tan or bone color. The Texas tortoise rarely digs a burrow; at most, it scoops out a shallow depression in the sand for protection. Like the desert tortoise, it feeds on grass, cactus pads, flowers, and fruit; sometimes it eats beetles and land snails.

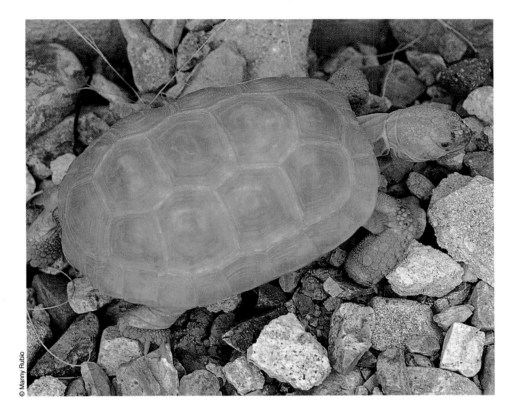

© Manny Rubio

Man is by far the chief destroyer of the Texas tortoise. Although the state of Texas has passed legislation protecting it from being harmed or taken as a pet, quite a few are still collected for the pet industry. This is unfortunate, because the species is only slightly more hardy than the desert and gopher tortoise, and it has a low reproductive potential, usually laying only one or two eggs per clutch.

The Bolson tortoise or giant Mexican gopher tortoise (*Gopherus flavomarginatus*), was only recently (1959) categorized as a separate species. It lives in a small region of north-central Mexico; typically, it may mature to about 1 foot (30 centimeters) in length, but a number of individuals have been recorded with a carapace length exceeding 2 feet (60 centimeters). It has a pale yellow or straw-colored carapace when young, turning pale brown in adults.

The Bolson tortoise digs burrows ranging from 10 to 20 feet (3 to 6 meters) long. Like the gopher tortoise, it feeds along grazing paths in the early morning and late afternoon, retiring to its burrow at midday and at night. Bolson tortoises are slowly being exterminated as people move onto the land or plant crops on the lands the tortoise inhabits. It is also hunted for food and sometimes killed simply because people think the tortoise competes with cattle for sparse grass.

Opposite page: California's state reptile, the desert tortoise *(Gopherus agassizi)* is now fully protected by legislation as an endangered species. *Above:* The desert tortoise is nomadic in its habits, traveling long distances from summer to winter to adapt to the extreme range of temperatures.

SIDE-NECKED TURTLES

The basic distinction between turtles depends on whether they retract their head straight back into their shell (straight-necked turtles) or by lateral flexion, laying it sideways in the groove between the carapace and plastron, next to a front foot (side-necks). These two groups (suborders) are known as Cryptodira and Pleurodira, respectively.

Most turtles in the world—the turtles we have been describing, nearly 150 species—belong to the suborder Cryptodira, or straight-necked turtles. No discussion of turtles would be complete, however, without a description of some of the two families (Pelomedusidae and Chelidae) and about sixty species that make up the suborder Pleurodira—the side-necked turtles. Some of the most unusual and interesting turtles in the world are side-necks.

Side-necked turtles are considered less physiologically advanced than straight-necked turtles, because a threatened side-necked turtle can only protect itself by pushing its head further into its shoulder, leaving one side of its neck and head exposed. The other major distinction between straight-necked and side-necked turtles is that the pelvic bones of side-necks are fused to both the carapace and plastron, while in straight-necked turtles there is no bony connection.

Seventy million years ago, side-necked turtles inhabited the globe on both sides of the equator. Today, they live only in the southern hemisphere—South America, sub-Saharan Africa, and Madagascar—and are the only non-marine turtles in Australia.

The largest of all side-necks of the family Pelomedusidae (five genera, about twenty-four species) is the arrau river turtle (*Podocnemis expansa*) which lives in the Amazon River system of South America.

The carapace of the arrau turtle is flat and brown, the plastron gray; the head is black with yellow markings and a pointed snout.

Large females grow to a carapace length of 3 feet (1 meter) and a weight of 200 pounds (75 kilograms), although the average size for females is 2 feet (73 centimeters) in length and 70 pounds (26 kilograms). Males are smaller and less numerous than females.

The arrau is similar in many respects to sea turtles; it is large and aquatic, it shows a preference for congregating at night in a few favored places to nest, and it lays many eggs (upward of 100). Also, like many sea turtles, arrau turtles may only nest every three or four years (though laying several clutches in that year). Adults are strictly herbivorous.

For more than 150 years, the arrau turtle has been heavily exploited by natives: Large numbers of adults are killed for food, and eggs are taken for food and other purposes (oil in the eggs is used for lighting, cooking, and lubrication).

In the past forty years, the arrau population has declined significantly: For example, it was estimated that in 1800, a favored nesting beach was used by 330,000 turtles;

in 1945, the number had dropped to 123,000; in 1956, to 36,000; and in 1969, to just under 14,000. The arrau river turtle is now an officially endangered species, but it is protected only sporadically.

Another prominent side-neck is the Amazon yellow-spotted turtle (*Podocnemis unifilis*). Somewhat similar in appearance to the arrau river turtle, the Amazon yellow-spotted turtle has a higher dome on its carapace and typically grows to a carapace length of about 15 inches (38 centimeters). It tends to inhabit ponds and lakes more than rivers.

More species of Pelomedusid side-necks live in Africa than anywhere else in the world. The side-neck with the greatest range is probably the helmeted turtle (*Pelomedusa subrufa*), which is found over most of the continent south of the Sahara. It has an olive-brown carapace and a yellowish plastron (though it lacks a plastral hinge); it typically grows to slightly less than a foot (36 centimeters) in length.

A gathering of teracays, or Amazon yellow-spotted turtles *(Podocnemis unifilis)*, a South American side-neck once popular in the pet trade.

North Wind Picture Archive

The helmeted turtle is semiaquatic, mostly carnivorous, and lays relatively large clutches of eggs (fifteen to forty). It likes to bask and has been observed doing so on the backs of hippopotamuses. The helmeted turtle was once heavily imported for the pet trade in Europe.

A number of other side-necked turtles live in sub-Saharan Africa. A dozen or so species belong to the genus *Pelusios,* which is distinguished by a hinge across the plastron, allowing the front portion to be raised as a protection for the head and forelimbs.

The other family of side-necked turtles, Chelidae, is composed of nine or ten genera and thirty-five to forty species, which are found in South America and Australia only. This family is considered more advanced than the Pelomedusidae, because parts of the carapace and skull are more specialized and resemble those of cryptodiran turtles.

Eight species of side-necks known as snake-necked turtles live in Australia. As their name suggests, snake-necked turtles have extremely long necks—sometimes the length of the head and neck is nearly that of the carapace. Snake-necked turtles are aquatic or semiaquatic.

The most familiar and widespread of the snake-necks is known simply as the Australian snake-necked turtle (*Chelodina longicollis*); it inhabits much of southwestern Australia (portions of the states of South Australia, Victoria, New South Wales, and Queensland). Adults grow to a carapace

An arrau river turtle, a large South American side-neck valued as a food source by native tribes.

length of about 7 inches (21 centimeters), with 12 inches (37 centimeters) as the maximum. Its shell is brown or black and has a wrinkled texture. The neck is dark on top, with a warty appearance; the head is slender, with a bright, staring eye, which gives it a bizarre, somewhat threatening look.

The Australian snake-necked turtle eats frogs, tadpoles, aquatic insects, and occasionally fish. When a newly caught turtle is picked up, it usually emits a strong-smelling liquid from glands near the rear legs. In captivity, however, the Australian snake-necked turtle becomes docile and friendly.

The largest of the Australian chelids is the snake-necked turtle known as *Chelodina expansa,* a river-dweller that lives in Queensland, New South Wales, and Victoria. It normally grows to a carapace length of 11 inches (34 centimeters); the largest specimens have been measured at nearly 17 inches (52 centimeters). The head of *C. expansa* is flat and wide; its diet is similar to that of *C. longicollis.*

Another snake-necked turtle worth mentioning is *Chelodina oblonga,* which lives in the swamps and streams of a large section of southwest Western Australia. Its neck is longer (relatively) than that of any other turtle species and is so thick and muscular that it is impossible for the turtle to draw it

© Bayard H. Brattstrom/Visuals Unlimited

into its shell. When the turtle walks, it holds its long neck and head straight out in front of the shell.

Another well-known Australian side-neck is the Murray River turtle (*Emydura macquarrii*), the most numerous species of its genus; it is found throughout the Murray River and its tributaries (in southern South Australia, New South Wales, and Victoria) and in other parts of western Australia.

The Murray River turtle grows to a maximum length of about 13 inches (40 centimeters); its relatively flat shell is very broad in juveniles, becoming oval as the animal matures. The shell is medium brown and has a wrinkled appearance. The Murray River turtle's head is small, with a pointed snout and bright, prominent eyes; usually, the head has a pair of barbels (cone-shaped projections) on the chin.

Frogs, tadpoles, and aquatic vegetation make up the Murray River turtle's diet. Apart from the fact that it is numerous, the most noteworthy quality about the Murray River turtle is its energetic, somewhat hostile temperament—it has an inclination to inflict painful bites on anyone attempting to capture or handle it. It is said to retain this disposition even in captivity.

Two species of snake-necked turtles are found in South America, although they belong to a different genus, *Hydromedusa*. The most plentiful and widely distributed is named *Hydromedusa tectifera,* a turtle that grows to a carapace length of 12 inches (36 centimeters) and inhabits parts of Argentina, Uruguay, Paraguay, and southern Brazil. Its carapace is dark brown or black, with a yellow-brown plastron. The top of the neck, head, and limbs is dark gray; the underside of the head is pale yellow with small, gray spots. Females grow to a larger size than males.

Little is known about the habits of *Hydromedusa tectifera*. It is said to be nervous and shy, retaining these qualities even in captivity. Its preferred food is snails, though it also eats tadpoles and aquatic insects.

Without a doubt, the most unusual turtle in the world—side-necked or straight-necked—is the famous matamata turtle (*Chelus fimbriatus*), an aquatic species that inhabits much of the Amazon and Orinoco river systems in northern South America.

© Erika Klass

The Australian matamata (*Chelus fimbriatus*), perhaps the most bizarre-looking turtle in the world.

So strange is the matamata that it barely looks like a turtle at all; it resembles a pile of debris. The matamata's carapace reaches a length of about 16 inches (49 centimeters), and the turtle has an extremely long, muscular neck. Its flattened, triangular head has a long snout, small eyes, and wide jaws with weak jaw muscles. Its limbs are small and weak.

The matamata's long carapace and neck is extremely rough and uneven in texture, and the head is covered with shreds and filaments of skin. Adult matamatas are dark brown or black, while younger turtles are often a more colorful brown and yellow mix, like fallen leaves. Adults often have a thick covering of algae on the carapace, which contributes to their camouflaged appearance.

The matamata leads a sedentary, but predatory, way of life, much like that of the alligator snapping turtle. It lies on the bottom of ponds and slow-moving streams and rivers, occasionally stretching its long neck to the surface to breathe. But mostly it just waits for small fish to come near; the fish nibble on fibrous parts of its head, thinking it to be edible refuse. Then the matamata springs into action, rapidly expanding its huge mouth and neck, sucking in a large flood of water and the hapless fish. Next, the matamata opens its mouth slightly and allows the water, but not the fish, to escape. Its jaws lack horny edges for chewing, so the matamata simply swallows its food whole.

MARINE TURTLES

A number of turtle species moved from the marshes and land back to the sea early on, about 150 million years ago. By 100 million years ago, four families of marine turtles inhabited the planet.

Marine turtles differ from semiaquatic turtles and tortoises in a number of their anatomical features. One of the most obvious is that the feet of marine turtles take the form of flippers—the digits are fused so the flippers function like efficient paddles, enabling marine turtles to move gracefully and rapidly through the water. Each flipper has only one or two claws, except for that of the leatherback, which has none.

Internally, the bony structure of the carapace and plastron is reduced in marine turtles, and the shell is streamlined. Marine turtles are unable to withdraw their necks and heads into their shells (to compensate, they have completely roofed-over skulls, which offer their vulnerable heads better protection). All species have glands that collect and excrete excessive salt from their blood.

Marine turtles inhabit all temperate and tropical oceans, spending virtually all their time in the water. Only female marine turtles leave the sea, when they come ashore to nest; a male may never leave the ocean in its entire lifetime—perhaps half a century. Because of this, we know relatively little of marine turtles' movements, navigational ability, or their development from infancy to maturity.

All species of marine turtles are capable of living on the high seas, and though some species (the green turtle, for instance) travel great distances between their feeding and nesting grounds, most spend the majority of their time in the warmer, shallower waters near the shorelines of continents and islands. This makes it easier to find food and mates. Only the leatherback and olive ridley spend much of their time in the open ocean.

Marine turtles eat both animal and vegetable foods. Seagrasses and algae are the most important vegetation; animal prey includes crabs, snails, jellyfish, mussels, and rarely small fish. All marine turtles are large (total length: 3 to 7 feet [1 to 2 meters]) and

© Gary Bell/Ellis Wildlife Collection

hence, as adults, have few enemies except man, although occasionally sharks or killer whales attack them.

The shells of adult marine turtles, with the exception of green turtles, typically become covered with all sorts of organisms, including seaweed, barnacles, crustaceans, and leeches. Remora—fish that frequently attach themselves by suction to sharks—also allow themselves to be carried along by marine turtles.

MIGRATION AND MATING

Over the past three decades, researchers have tagged marine turtles with metal or plastic identification markers in an attempt to chart their patterns of migration. They have learned that turtles migrate between specific beaches and feeding grounds.

What we do not understand is how turtles that migrate over great stretches of open ocean find their way from place to place. For instance, how does a female green turtle find her way back to the beach where she was hatched decades before, so that she may lay her eggs? As Pritchard says, "... the feat of locating Ascension Island, barely seven miles across, after negotiating 1,400 miles of open ocean, by an animal that is hopelessly myopic when it raises its eyes above the level of the water, seems little short of miraculous."

Scientists think that the turtle's senses of smell, taste, and sight must be involved:

The loggerhead (Caretta caretta) is so named for its relatively large head. It is found in the Atlantic, Pacific, and Indian oceans, as well as the Mediterranean Sea.

Hatchlings smell or nibble the sand on their way to the nest, as if attempting to imprint its scent or taste upon their senses. Likewise, adult green turtles and ridleys appear to test the sand when they crawl onto a beach to nest. Perhaps, like bees, turtles have a sun-compass sense and are able to use the sun and stars to guide themselves—we just don't know.

Marine turtles mate offshore, then the females emerge from the sea to lay their eggs. Depending on the species, a turtle may nest up to six times (at two-week intervals) in a season, mating in between nestings. Many marine turtles rarely nest every year—two- to three-year intervals are typical.

Nesting generally takes place at night. Females drag themselves out of the surf and move laboriously as much as 100 yards (91 meters) up the beach, out of reach of the highest tides. Initially, many species are very skittish and will return to the sea at the slightest noise or sound.

When she has selected a site, she begins to dig a nest with her hind flippers in the more densely packed sand under her tail. While she is digging, "tears" flow from her eyes to eliminate excess salt from her system and wash away any sand that has accumulated.

Depending on the size of the turtle, the egg cavity might be from 1 to 2½ feet (36 to 91 centimeters) deep. Once the nest has been dug, the female lays her eggs—each about 2

inches (6 centimeters) in diameter, anywhere from fifty to 200 in number—singly or in groups of three or four, in intervals of eight to twelve seconds. She folds her flippers up out of the way and lets the eggs drop directly onto the sand.

The total egg-laying process usually takes from fifteen to thirty minutes. At this time, females are especially vulnerable, because once a turtle begins laying her eggs, almost nothing can dissuade her, even the presence of people or predators. She is in an almost trancelike state, focused only on this. To complete the process, the turtle covers the nest with sand, flinging it around with both flippers and flattening the whole area with her body.

Afterward, it is difficult to determine the location of the nest itself. Then, often nearly exhausted, the female drags herself—perhaps pausing several times to rest—to the surf and disappears into the ocean.

Predators (human beings, coyotes, wild dogs, and feral hogs) seem to know when and where turtles will come ashore to nest, and they await the turtles' arrival. As well, humans take the eggs and sometimes kill the turtles as they are nesting.

Additionally, humans and killer whales often attack male and female turtles while they are mating. Raccoons and skunks, using their sense of smell, destroy nests and eat the eggs. If a turtle's nest can survive a couple of days, though, the female's scent usually diminishes sufficiently and the nest is safe.

After varying periods of incubation (two to two-and-a-half months is typical), baby turtles burst from the nest, usually at night. Focusing on the reflection of light off the water, they head for the sea. Again, the predators—gulls, ravens, ghost crabs, sharks, groupers—are there, waiting for a meal of young turtles. Many are eaten in the first few days of life.

Once in the water, the hatchlings enter what are referred to as "the lost years," that indeterminate period of time when humans rarely see them. On one occasion in the late 1980s, near the end of his life, Archie Carr watched dozens of newly hatched sea turtles scramble from their nest and dash pell-mell toward the ocean, vanishing in the surf. "Where are they going?" he said. "I wish I

The largest and most widely distributed of the hard-shell marine turtles, the green turtle (*Chelonia mydas*) is famous for its extensive migrations.

© Dr. E.R. Degginger

© Chris Huss/Ellis Wildlife Collection

knew. I've spent a lot of time working on that problem, and so have a lot of other people."

Turtle experts think that, somehow, most hatchlings make their way to rafts of seaweed and sargassum, feeding and drifting with the currents until they become large enough and strong enough to travel through the ocean. How many survive to maturity? Estimates vary: A reasonable guess is one per thousand.

THE SEVEN SPECIES

Currently, there are two families of marine turtles: Cheloniidae, with six species (the green turtle, flatback, loggerhead, hawksbill, Kemp's ridley and olive ridley); and Dermochelyidae, with a single species (the leatherback).

The most abundant of marine turtles is the green turtle (*Chelonia mydas*), which inhabits the Atlantic, Pacific, and Indian oceans, plus the Mediterranean Sea. Its primary nesting beaches are located in Central

and South America, Asia, Australia, Indonesia, Hawaii, Ascension Island (in the Atlantic Ocean), and Europa Island (near Madagascar).

As mentioned above, green turtles are famous for their extensive migrations; for example, green turtles who feed off the coast of Brazil swim to Ascension Island, 1,400 miles (2,240 kilometers) away, to make their nests.

The green turtle is the largest of the hardshell marine turtles. Typically it grows to a carapace length of about 40 inches (1 meter) and a weight of 300 to 350 pounds (110 to 130 kilograms), although individuals measuring about 55 inches (1.7 meters) and weighing close to 500 pounds (187 kilograms) have been recorded.

The carapace of the green turtle is smooth, heart-shaped, and, in adults, medium brown or olive in color; the green turtle gets its name from the color of its calipee (belly cartilage), which is used to make turtle soup. The plastron is light yellow, its head is small, its snout is rounded, and its eyes are prominent.

The green turtle (*Chelonia mydas*) is the largest of the hardshelled sea turtles. Found in all oceans, the green turtle has been called "the archetypical marine turtle" by Peter Pritchard and "the most valuable reptile in the world " by Archie Carr.

The green turtle feeds mostly on sea-grasses and marine algae. Its serrated lower jaw is well-suited for this, but it also has been reported to eat crustaceans, jellyfish, and sponges. Juveniles may be more carnivorous than adults.

Green turtle meat and eggs have been an important source of food for native populations; Europeans and Americans consider green turtle steaks a delicacy. As a result, whole populations of green turtles have been decimated, and today the species is classified as endangered by the IUCN *Red Data Book*.

At one time, for instance, the green turtle nested in great numbers on beaches in Florida, but now in the United States only a handful of females nest on a small section of beach in Florida. In Indonesia, 36 million eggs were collected in 1936; between 1967 and 1972, the average number taken was only 320,000.

The flatback turtle (*Natator depressus*), lives off the beaches of northern Australia. The flatback is small (typically: 30 inches [91 centimeters] and 160 pounds [60 kilograms]) and has a flattened carapace with turned-up edges. Its head is relatively larger and more triangularly shaped than that of the green turtle, and its front flippers are relatively shorter.

Little is known of the flatback's behavior, migrations, or feeding habits. It lays fewer eggs (fifty in a typical clutch) than any other marine turtle, but the eggs are larger than those of any but the leatherback's, to which they are equal in size. Pritchard says that this gives the flatback hatchlings, which are 50 percent larger than green turtle or loggerhead hatchlings, a better chance of surviving attacks by gulls and ghost crabs. Monitor lizards and foxes destroy flatback nests.

Another large marine turtle is the loggerhead (*Caretta caretta*), which is named for its large, broad head. Loggerheads typically grow to a carapace length of 3 feet (1 meter) and a weight of 200 to 350 pounds (75 to 130 kilograms). Its carapace is reddish brown, and its plastron is yellow-orange.

Loggerheads live in the Atlantic (nesting in Florida), the Mediterranean, the Indian Ocean (off southern Africa and Madagascar), and the Pacific (near Japan, China, Australia, and Mexico).

Typically, the loggerhead nests far from rather than close to the equator: just north of the Tropic of Cancer and just south of the Tropic of Capricorn. Like the green turtle, the loggerhead is an extensive traveler.

Loggerheads are omnivorous, but prefer a diet of meat: crabs, conches, urchins, jellyfish, squid, barnacles, sponges, and fish. They will, however, eat small quantities of seaweed. Loggerheads are reputed to be hostile and aggressive when captured, capable of inflicting considerable damage on fishing boats and their crews.

At one time, loggerheads were prized for their meat and eggs. This is still true in some underdeveloped countries, but in many developed countries, including the United States, the species is listed as threatened and is therefore protected. Today, the largest single cause of loggerhead mortality is accidental drowning in shrimp trawls.

The hawksbill (*Eretmochelys imbricata*) gets its name from its long, narrow head and snout, which tapers to a point. It lives mostly in tropical waters—the Caribbean (Cuba, Panama, and Costa Rica), north of Madagascar, Indonesia, and off the northeast coast of Australia.

Smaller than the green turtle, flatback, and loggerhead, the hawksbill varies in size depending on where it is found. Those in the Caribbean typically grow to a carapace length of 2½ to 3 feet (76 to 91 centimeters) and weigh from 100 to 165 pounds (45 to 75 kilograms); Asian and Pacific hawksbills range in size from 2 to 2½ feet (61 to 76 centimeters) and 75 to 110 pounds (28 to 41 kilograms). The carapace of the hawksbill is heart-shaped, like that of the green turtle, and ranges in color from amber to dark brown or dark green. The head and limbs are dark brown or black on the upper surfaces; underneath, they are whitish yellow or yellow-orange, as is the plastron.

The hawksbill is omnivorous, though it prefers a diet of marine invertebrates, such as mollusks, crustaceans, sea urchins, jellyfish, and sponges. Young hawksbills are generally herbivorous, becoming more carnivorous as they mature.

On the average, hawksbills lay more eggs than other sea turtles, about 160 per clutch in Caribbean nests. Unlike some other marine species, which nest in large numbers, hawksbills frequently nest alone or in small groups. This makes it difficult to learn much about their habits and behavior.

Opposite page: The loggerhead *(Caretta caretta)* has a long, reddish brown carapace and a large head.
Overleaf: One of the smaller sea turtles, the hawksbill *(Eretmochelys imbricata)* is prized for its colorful scutes, the source of tortoiseshell products. Juveniles are also stuffed and mounted as decoration for homes and offices in the Orient.

© Manny Rubio

A green turtle (Chelonia mydas [top of photo]) and a hawksbill (bottom of photo).

Although it is eaten only infrequently, the hawksbill is prized the world over for its beautiful scutes, known incorrectly as "tortoiseshell." Thick and overlapping, the horny scutes are translucent with radiating streaks of reddish brown and black when peeled from the carapace and polished.

Juvenile hawksbills are imported to Japan from Indonesia, where they are stuffed, lacquered, and hung on the walls of many Japanese residences, ironically as a symbol of longevity. About 10,000 young hawksbills per year meet this fate in the Orient, and the same practice takes place in Mexico. The hawksbill is considered endangered, and Pritchard describes the species as "universally heavily exploited."

The smallest, rarest, and most endangered of marine turtles is the Kemp's ridley (*Lepidochelys kempii*), which lives only in the Gulf of Mexico and the shallow, coastal waters of the eastern United States. It has a broad carapace that seldom grows beyond a length of 2½ feet (76 centimeters) and a weight of 80 to 120 pounds (30 to 45 kilograms). The carapace, skin, and plastron are gray in hatchlings, but as the turtle matures, the plastron, neck, and underside of the shoulders become pale yellow and the carapace sometimes becomes olive green.

Kemp's ridleys prefer a largely carnivorous diet, eating crabs, shrimp, clams, lobster, jellyfish, and snails.

The Kemp's ridley is reputed to respond with extreme violence and hysteria when attempts are made to capture it, thrashing and snapping itself to exhaustion. In captivity, Kemp's ridleys become more calm but never entirely lose their nervous dispositions.

The most unusual quality about the Kemp's ridley is its nesting behavior, which was unknown to the scientific world until 1963. It nests primarily in one place in the world, on a remote beach near the village of Rancho Nuevo in Tamaulipas, Mexico, about 200 miles (320 kilometers) south of Brownsville, Texas. Ridleys gather in the waters offshore and swarm onto the beach all at the same time, during the day (rather than at night, when most marine turtles nest).

This event, known locally as an *arribada* (arrival or aggregation), takes place three times a season, at intervals of a few weeks in the months of April through June, on a slightly different section of beach each time.

Mexican natives have known about arribadas for a long time; the event serves as a convenient way for them to obtain turtle meat and eggs. The outside world learned of arribadas by accident, however. A local resident, Andres Herrera, filmed an arribada in 1947, but only a few people ever saw the film until more than a decade later. It shows thousands of turtles coming ashore; the best estimate is that perhaps 40,000 nested in a single day.

An indication of how much the Kemp's ridley has been exploited in recent years is the fact that although the Mexican government has protected the arribadas against poachers since 1966, sometimes with armed soldiers, the population of nesting Kemp's ridleys continues to decline. In recent years, only about 400 females per season have come to Rancho Nuevo to nest.

The other largest single enemy of the Kemp's ridley is the shrimp trawler—750 Kemp's ridleys per year are drowned in shrimpers' nets.

Slightly larger than the Kemp's ridley is the olive ridley (*Lepidochelys olivacea*), which inhabits tropical waters of the Pacific, Indian, and South Atlantic oceans. It has a thinner, narrower carapace that is uniformly olive in color, and a smaller, more lightly built skull with less-muscular jaws. Unlike Kemp's ridleys, olive ridleys do not restrict themselves just to coastal waters, but rather swim far out into the ocean. The diet of the olive ridley is similar to that of the Kemp's ridley, except that it does not include as many hard-shelled invertebrates.

Olive ridleys, too, participate in arribadas, though they generally nest at night. Nesting sites are located in the south Atlantic in Surinam and Costa Rica, at several locations on the west coast of Mexico, and on the coast at Orissa, India. Nesting takes place in almost every month of the year, depending on location. The largest arribada on record occurred in 1968, on the Pacific coast at Escobilla, Oaxaca, Mexico, and involved an estimated 80,000 turtles.

Several decades ago, Mexican natives heavily exploited the eggs of the olive ridley and its population began to decline. Now, because it is listed as a threatened species, the turtle and its eggs are protected.

The largest marine turtle—in fact, the largest reptile in the world—is the leatherback (*Dermochelys coriacea*). It is so markedly different from other sea turtles in its physiology (though not in its habits) that it is placed in another family, Dermochelyidae, of which it is the sole species.

The most obvious difference about the leatherback is that its huge, barrel-shaped body has no shell; instead, it has a leathery, scaleless skin over a thick, greasy layer of cartilage, in which is imbedded a mosaic of thousands of small, polygonal bones.

The leatherback has paddlelike, clawless flippers; massive, muscular shoulders and neck; a large, smooth head with relatively weak, scissorlike jaws; and tender skin on its neck and legs. Males have concave plastrons, slightly depressed, tapering carapaces, and tails that are considerably longer than those of females.

The leatherback's carapace is black, with longitudinal ridges. Its whitish plastron also has five longitudinal ridges. The head and limbs are the same color as the carapace. Sometimes the carapace and flippers are dotted with white spots. Leatherbacks grow to a carapace length of 5 to 7 feet (1.5 to 2 meters) and a weight of 700 to 1,600 pounds (260 to 600 kilograms). The largest leatherback recorded, a male, washed up on a beach in Wales in 1988; it weighed 2,016 pounds (750 kilograms).

Except for its nesting activity, very little is known of the migrations, diet, and behavior of the leatherback. An accomplished deep-sea swimmer, it is the most wide-ranging of marine turtles. Leatherbacks have been spotted in all oceans, frequently far out of sight of land; sometimes leatherbacks travel in groups of up to 100 turtles.

Although for the most part it inhabits temperate and tropical waters, the leatherback has the metabolic capacity to raise its body temperature above that of the water it swims in, enabling it to inhabit waters too cold for other marine turtles (for instance, off the coasts of Iceland, Canada, and Argentina). It is not known whether leatherbacks migrate or simply roam the seas. Leatherbacks specialize on a diet of jellyfish.

Leatherbacks nest at various times on beaches all over the world: both coasts of Florida, Jamaica, French Guiana, Nicaragua, Costa Rica, and on the west coast of South Africa in the Atlantic; Natal, Ceylon, India, Thailand, Malaysia, Australia, and Mexico in the Pacific. Nesting takes place individually or in small groups. During a season, leatherbacks lay eggs, on the average, more frequently than other sea turtles (as many as nine times, at ten-day intervals), though the clutch size is generally smaller (50 to 120 eggs).

Because the leatherback is such a wide-ranging "loner," it's hard to estimate how many exist. Population estimates have been revised upward in recent years, and it is now thought that there are as many as 120,000 nesting females alive. However, the fact that there seems to be an increase in the leatherback population may have more to do with the discovery of more nesting sites than with an increase in the numbers of actual turtles.

The species is still heavily exploited for its oil, although there are satisfactory synthetic substitutes for every use to which the oil is put (cosmetics, lighting, etc.). Additionally, many leatherbacks have died in recent years from intestinal blockage; it appears they have mistaken plastic bags floating in the ocean for jellyfish.

Leatherbacks do not survive in captivity. Adult leatherbacks struggle violently against any attempts at capture, smashing themselves into the sides of cages and tanks until they die. Even leatherbacks raised from hatchlings only live a year or so, at most. This most majestic of marine turtles is presently considered an endangered species.

TURTLES
AND
HUMANS

A TANGLED HISTORY

onsidered historically and cross-culturally, the attitudes of human beings toward turtles have been widely varied and inconsistent. People have studied turtles; kept them as pets; venerated them; eaten their flesh and made use of their eggs, oil, and skin; ignored them; labored in their behalf; and thoughtlessly abused and exploited them.

We have treated turtles, alternately, as respected fellow creatures of the Earth and, to borrow an expression from Shakespeare, as "blocks, stones, and worse than senseless things." For their part, turtles have left us alone, asking nothing except to be allowed to live their lives undisturbed.

In his book *Reptiles,* Archie Carr said: "It has taken some 150 million years of paleontological disasters to reduce the immense diversity of reptilian life to a meager four orders. But it has taken man only a few hundred years of indiscriminate slaughtering to bring many survivors to the brink of complete extinction." This statement certainly applies to a significant number of turtle species.

This chapter will assess the present state of affairs between turtles and humans. On a superficial level, of course, that seems a simple enough undertaking, because in our relations with turtles we hold power over their lives, not the other way around. For us, it is natural to see the situation entirely from our perspective, describing how we view turtles and how we act toward them.

On a deeper level, however, turtles have a certain power over us: the power to reveal us as we really are, to make crystal-clear the

TURTLES IN MYTH AND FOLKLORE

way we see ourselves and the planet we live on, the quality of life we will bequeath to future generations, and perhaps even our very prospects for survival.

At one time or another, the turtle has been a part of the cultural history of people in every part of the globe turtles live. Turtle images appeared on Greek coins six centuries before the birth of Christ; today, they are found on postage stamps around the world.

Turtles have played a part in the religious and artistic traditions of many cultures, too, particularly in China, Japan, and India, where turtles are represented in paintings and in sculpture.

Perhaps of even greater significance is that turtles form an important part of the folklore and myths of many societies, the psychosocial foundations from which the world view of a culture is derived.

In ancient myths and legends, the turtle is almost always greatly revered as a symbol of strength, stability, benevolence, and wisdom. Perhaps the oldest legend—in which the turtle is considered to be the second incarnation of the powerful god Vishnu—comes from India and Hinduism.

After a great flood, which occurs every four billion years and dissolves the Earth, Vishnu transforms himself into a great turtle. On his back by sheer force of will, he supports the vessel in which the gods and demons mix the elements necessary to re-create the globe. After a thousand years, when the Earth has been reborn, the turtle remains in place, and on his back stands a large elephant (or four smaller elephants, in some versions), which support the planet.

In the folklore of ancient China, Kwei, the dragon turtle, first emerged after the world was destroyed to restore order, taking charge of the creation of the heavens and earth, which required some 18,000 years. He then passed his life on to a series of guardian turtles, who were instructed to help mankind pursue truth and wisdom.

In another Chinese myth, an immense turtle actually became the world, which is contained within its body: The interior of its plastron contained the oceans upon which the continents of the Earth float, and its great, vaulted carapace formed the dome of the heavens, complete with stars and planets.

Native Americans shared the reverence felt for the turtle by Asian cultures. In fact, Native American tribes have probably created the greatest number of folk tales in which the turtle plays an important part in cosmological matters. For many tribes, the land on which they lived was the carapace of a huge "mother turtle," floating in a vast, primal sea. Almost every tribe in North America regarded one species of turtle or another as sacred. According to Archie Carr, only the Creeks took exception: They thought that box turtles caused droughts and floods, and killed them on sight.

In Central America, the Mayans gave special status to turtles, which were linked to their astronomical and mathematical systems. The Mayans depended on agriculture for their survival, and they believed that the turtle brought rain to make the crops grow. Because they observed turtles survive forest fires unharmed, the Mayans also thought that turtles have a supernatural talent for survival.

In ancient times, Egyptians generally considered the turtle to be sacred, although the Egyptian tradition apparently contained inconsistencies: In some time periods, turtles were anathema, creatures of watery darkness—the opposite of the sun god, Ra. As such, they were not to be eaten or used in any medicines; an epithet of the time stated: "May Ra live and the turtle die."

Ancient Greeks regarded the turtle as sacred and even believed that their gods felt the same way. Of course, the legendary Greek storyteller, Aesop, is given credit for the well-known fable in which a tortoise, through determination and wisdom, wins a race with a hare.

In modern times, few cultures accord the turtle any special significance. It is still held as sacred among some Asian peoples, however. One of the best-known examples is the turtles living at the Buddhist temple complex known as Wat Po, in Bangkok, Thailand. Many turtles, mostly *Hieremys annandalei,* a large black emydid turtle, live in the waters surrounding the temple.

Visitors feed fruit and vegetables to the turtles, which are regarded as symbols of immortality. The turtles are considered to be temporary dwelling places for the human souls as they make their way through a series of existences on the path to Nirvana. A similar colony of softshells (*Trionyx nigricans*) in Chittagong, Bangladesh, has already been mentioned (see page 54), although there is disagreement as to its symbolic significance.

Today, the principal interest humans have in turtles is practical or utilitarian. For example, natives living on the islands of the Seychelles Archipelago, off Madagascar in the Indian Ocean, present a newborn child with a giant Aldabran tortoise. The tortoise is raised until the child marries, then is killed and served at the wedding feast.

A Micronesian native hauls away a sea turtle to be slaughtered.

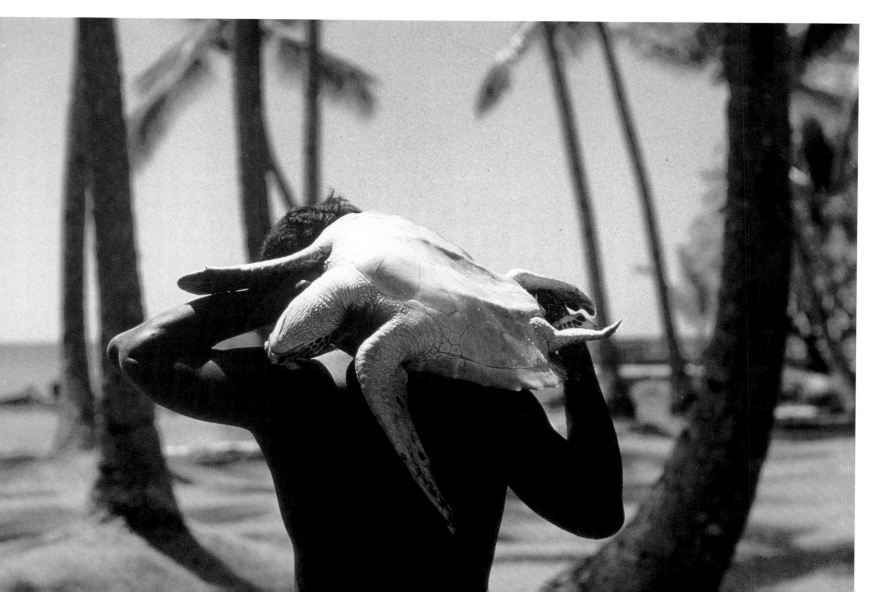

HUMAN BEINGS AND TURTLES TODAY

Turtles the world over, particularly marine turtles, are disappearing rapidly for a number of reasons: a continuing demand for turtle meat and eggs; a thriving market for tortoiseshell and leather products; accidental catching by shrimp trawlers; destruction and overdevelopment of nesting grounds by humans; and environmental pollution.

When considering the state of affairs between humans and turtles, the issue under discussion is not an ethical one: Do humans have the right to use turtles for their own purposes—to kill them, eat their flesh and eggs, and turn their skin and shells into clothing and various decorative items? That's a legitimate, but separate, question. Rather, the issue is: What constitutes rational use, and what constitutes abuse? And further: Apart from use (and overuse), what other human actions pose the greatest threat to turtles? Which species are in the most danger? What are the consequences of exploitation, and what efforts are being made to save turtles from being exploited?

TURTLES AS FOOD

More than any other reptile, the turtle has been used by humans for food, and archaeological excavations indicate that this has been true for at least 20,000 years. Today, the turtle is unknown as food—or is consumed as a luxury or a novelty—in much of the Western world, but in many pre-industrial societies, turtle meat and eggs are staples and important sources of protein.

Marine and river turtles are eaten worldwide; they are hunted with bows and arrows, spears, harpoons, and nets. Tortoises, too, are taken universally for food; as Peter Pritchard points out, they "have a unique, and for them, disastrous combination of characteristics; they are . . . excellent to eat, ridiculously easy to catch, and with virtually no way of defending themselves."

In third world countries, people usually take only enough turtles and eggs to meet their immediate needs; their harvesting generally has not negatively affected local turtle populations on a long-term basis. For many of these people, the object of turtle hunting is survival. Or, as Fritz Obst succinctly puts it in *Turtles, Tortoises and Terrapins*: ". . . it is not the utilization of the creatures by primitive races that leads to their extinction, but the immoderate intervention of profit-seeking 'civilized' nations into the life and nature of tropical countries and their peoples."

For example, in the mid-nineteenth century, a European explorer, Walter Henry Bates, spent eleven years in the Amazon River basin; his book, *The Naturalist on the River Amazons,* published in 1863, describes how settlers and natives hunted turtles. Turtles (particularly the arrau river turtle) were killed for their meat, and their eggs were taken for oil, which was used for cooking and lighting; this practice had been carried on by the natives for hundreds of years.

With the coming of settlers from Europe, who persuaded natives to collect oil to sell for profit, the situation changed as the demand for oil skyrocketed. Based on the number of containers of oil collected in a year, and knowing how many eggs were needed to supply the contents of one container, Bates estimated that the total number of eggs destroyed amounted to 48 million in a single year.

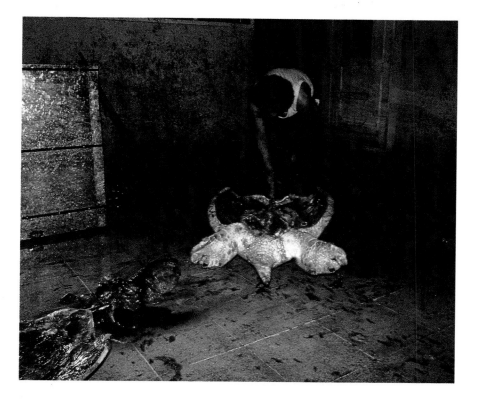

Above: The remains of poached green turtles, found at the Sea of Cortez, Baja California.
Right: A sea turtle slaughterhouse, Costa Rica.

Excessive egg-collecting in the Amazon continued to the extent that in this century the arrau turtle became a critically endangered species. And of course, the destruction of the giant tortoises of the Galapagos Islands and the islands off Madagascar provide another extreme illustration of Obst's statement.

Today, the turtles whose existence has been most threatened by the demand for their meat, skin, and shells are the big marine turtles. An account of their treatment serves to illustrate what is happening, in less dramatic ways, to other species of turtles all over the world because it results from the same shortsightedness and disregard.

The most frequently killed marine turtle, though not the most endangered (that dubious honor belongs to the Kemp's ridley) is the green turtle. Exploitation of the green turtle began in the mid-1600s, when the British colony at Jamaica sent ships to the Cayman Islands in the West Indies—considered by some to be the largest green turtle breeding grounds that have ever existed—to bring back turtle meat to feed the colony. By 1688, ships were carrying 13,000 turtles a year to Jamaica, and green turtle meat became the most frequently eaten meat there.

Laws prohibiting the collection of turtle eggs on any island belonging to Jamaica were enacted (but apparently not enforced) in the early 1700s. By the late 1700s, only a few turtles nested in the Caymans, and by 1840 ships were forced to travel all the way to the Miskito Cays off Nicaragua to obtain green turtles. By 1900, the nesting population in the Cayman Islands had been completely wiped out.

A brief history of the Miskito people of the eastern coast of Nicaragua, who hunt the green turtle, provides an excellent illustration of the ways which, in the modern world, economic and environmental concerns can become entangled to threaten both a human community and a species' existence.

For hundreds of years, the Miskito hunted the green turtle from open boats with harpoons; they became known as the best turtle hunters of the Caribbean. When they returned with the catch, the hunters shared turtle meat with the community in a ritual ceremony. In addition to turtle hunting, the Miskito provided for themselves by hunting and subsistence farming.

When Europeans came to Central America, they needed meat and were willing to pay the Miskito for it, first with goods, later with money. As agriculture, mining, and logging developed in Nicaragua, there was likewise an increasing demand for turtle meat, which the Miskito, abandoning their other economic activities, provided.

In short, the Miskito became dependent on, and victims of, a cash economy. As other industries shut down, their situation became more desperate; they were forced to spend more time hunting for turtles. In the 1960s, foreign concerns "helped" the Miskito by setting up turtle-processing plants and providing company boats and nets to increase the take of turtles.

The result is that the green turtle has become increasingly scarce as the Miskito have become more dependent on it for their livelihood. The social bonding produced by the ceremonial distribution of turtle flesh has been destroyed, and the Miskito now must sell turtles for

A false map turtle hatching.

© A.B. Sheldon

cash to buy food: flour, rice, beans, sugar, and coffee. And when the turtles become so scarce that it no longer makes economic sense to hunt them, what will the Miskito do? In this scenario, both the Miskito and the green turtle have become losers.

Overhunting has affected other species as well. Once the arribadas of the Kemp's ridley at Tamaulipas became well known in the early 1960s, there was a wholesale slaughter of adults and collecting of eggs for almost half a decade. Finally, the Mexican government took measures to protect the turtles from poachers by using soldiers armed with submachine guns to patrol beaches.

As an indication of how thorough the plundering was, for a few years pack trains of forty to fifty burros were used to haul the eggs away, and from the 40,000 females that nested in the early 1960s, the numbers dwindled to about 4,000 turtles in the 1970s; today, only about 400 females remain. "Even with twenty years of good beach protection the species is declining, disappearing off the face of the Earth," Archie Carr said in an interview in the late 1980s.

The arribadas of the olive ridley at Escobilla Beach, Oaxaca, on the southwestern shore of Mexico, too, have been heavily raided. Hundreds of thousands of turtles have been killed there in the 1980s, and the number of nesting females has been reduced from a high of nearly 100,000 per year in 1968 to about 20,000 in the mid-1980s. The Mexican government has made a dedicated effort to protect both turtles and their nests against poachers by levying quotas and patrol-

The wasted remains of a slaughtered sea turtle, probably poached.

A loggerhead lays her eggs near the Great Barrier Reef in Australia.

© Gerry Ellis/Ellis Wildlife Collection

ing beaches, but the coastline is long and the resources for enforcement sometimes have been scarce.

Another consequence of killing too many turtles and taking too many eggs is that the maximum size of individual specimens has declined. At the beginning of the twentieth century it was not unusual to catch green turtles approaching a half-ton in size, but presently 300-pound (112-kilogram) specimens are considered unusually large.

Compared to the wholesale slaughter of sea turtles, the killing of turtles for food by North Americans and Europeans has had a less significant impact on turtle populations, though it has not been inconsiderable. At different times in the past century, the diamond-back terrapin population has been variously threatened, and alligator snappers have become scarcer as well.

DEMAND FOR TORTOISESHELL AND TURTLE SKIN

Worldwide trade in commercial sea turtle products has increased continuously throughout this century. A recent public television special, *Sea Turtles: Ancient Nomads,* stated that there is more profit to be made from sea turtle products than any other category of animal on earth, and as a result, several turtle species are nearly extinct.

The most affected species are the hawksbill (for the layered scutes on its carapace, from which tortoiseshell is made) and the olive ridley (for its skin, from which turtle leather is made). To a lesser extent, the green turtle is also killed for tortoiseshell. Tortoiseshell and turtle-leather products include bracelets, decorative combs, inlays, belts, shoes, and handbags.

Three of the nations most heavily involved in producing products made from turtle shells and skin are Japan, Mexico, and Indonesia. According to Michael Weber, vice president of the Center for Marine Conservation, Japanese trade in sea turtle products has cost the lives of two million sea turtles since 1970. (One hawksbill yields up to twelve pounds [four kilograms] of tortoiseshell.)

In 1980, according to one estimate, raw tortoiseshell was selling for $45 a pound in Japan, and 45,000 pounds were being imported annually for that country's crafts industry. Other sources estimate the amount imported annually into Japan at closer to 100,000 pounds, up from 14,000 pounds per year in the early 1960s.

For many Japanese, turtles are a symbol of luck and prosperity, which explains the attraction of tortoiseshell products. It is said, for example, that a Japanese bride who doesn't have a tortoiseshell comb in her hair when she marries is bound to have misfortune. The annual use by the Japanese of nearly 9,000 lacquered, stuffed juvenile hawksbills as wall decorations already has been noted. In the mid-1980s, Indonesia was sending 28,000 hawksbills annually to Japan for processing.

Mexico and Ecuador harvested some 150,000 olive ridleys in 1979, primarily for their skins. This is an additional sad fact of "turtle economics"; frequently, the skin is what is considered valuable (only the flippers and skin of the neck is used) and turtle hunters throw the rest of the turtle overboard or leave it to rot on the beach.

Meanwhile, the turtle continues to become more scarce. The people of Indonesia, like the Miskito, have become entangled in the web of a cash economy. Efforts at conservation have been largely for naught; for those who hunt the hawksbill, it is often the best work they can find in areas where high unemployment is chronic.

Those who benefit most from the tortoiseshell and turtleskin trade are the wholesalers, and for them considerations of greed far outweigh any concern for the welfare of the turtles. Their attitude is that they will take all they can now, and when this resource is exhausted, they will turn to something else. "The trade in sea turtles is well-documented and grim," said Michael Weber. "Indonesia could take preventive measures, but it is shipping off its future to Japan."

The irony of the trade in tortoiseshell and turtle skin, of course, is that they are used entirely to make luxury products, and in every instance substitutes, many appearing almost identical to the genuine item, are available.

Every year, 45,000 turtles, mostly loggerheads, are caught as "by-catch," along with tons of unwanted fish, in the nets of the 10,000 to 15,000 shrimp trawlers operating in the ocean waters off the southeastern United States. For every pound of shrimp obtained, ten pounds of fish and other bycatch are netted.

Because nets sometimes are dragged for hours before they are brought up, one in four trapped turtles drowns—more than 11,000 loggerheads annually, the largest single source of loggerhead mortality in the United States.

Trawlers also account for the deaths of about 750 Kemp's ridleys per year. "Far and away the most direct and injurious [threat against the Kemp's ridley] is the take by shrimp trawlers," Archie Carr said in the mid-1980s.

Fortunately, there is a simple, inexpensive solution to this problem. Developed over the past dozen years, it's known as the turtle excluder device—TED, for short. When attached to shrimp nets, TEDS allow turtles and up to 70 percent of the unwanted fish bycatch to pass through while still trapping shrimp, according to the U.S. Fish and Wildlife Service.

Dr. Peter Pritchard, one of the world's leading authorities on turtles, measures a leatherback.

DEATH IN SHRIMPERS' NETS

Though even accidental killing of an endangered species is against the law, shrimpers have steadfastly resisted the use of TEDS, claiming that they let up to one-third of the shrimp pass through the nets. Although TEDS are inexpensive ($250–$400) and funds have been made available to purchase them, shrimpers consider them a nuisance. In 1987, less than 1 percent of the shrimp boats in operation employed TEDs.

"If TEDs aren't used, the Kemp's ridley will disappear within ten years," said Archie Carr. Apparently, the United States government agreed: Legislation was passed that required all commercial shrimp trawlers to use TEDs by mid-1989. In South Carolina, during the first two weeks of July 1989, turtle deaths were down dramatically after TEDS were put into use: Only six turtles were drowned, compared with an average of fifty-six during the same period over the previous nine years.

Shrimpers protested the regulations, however, blockading ports in Texas and Louisiana. This caused Commerce Secretary Robert Mosbacher to accede to the demands of shrimpers and politicians: On July 24 he suspended the regulations requiring the use of TEDs for forty-five days, ignoring the advice of scientific experts and Department of Commerce lawyers in the process. Politicians from Texas and Louisiana had argued that utilizing the TEDs was "shortsighted" and "would close out the livelihood of thousands of shrimpers."

Mosbacher proposed an alternative: hauling up the shrimp nets every 105 minutes in order to release any turtles caught during that time, despite evidence from the Coast Guard that almost all shrimpers were ignoring the rule.

Reaction from environmental groups was immediate and uncompromising. The National Wildlife Federation filed suit seeking a restraining order against Mosbacher's proposal, and on September 5, 1989, Mosbacher reversed his position, stating that the TEDs must be implemented. "This is a final decision on our part," spokesman Brian Gorman of the Commerce Department said.

DESTRUCTION AND OVERDEVELOPMENT OF NESTING GROUNDS

Turtles tend to nest on very expensive pieces of real estate. The loggerhead provides an excellent case in point. The largest loggerhead nesting grounds in the western Atlantic are on the beaches of six counties on the east coast of Florida; female loggerheads make about 10,000 nests there annually.

The problem is that these nests are very close to resorts and other centers of human population, and when the loggerhead hatchlings emerge, they often mistake the lights from inland for the ocean. Many head in the wrong direction, to be captured by predators, die from exposure to the sun, or be smashed by cars as they scurry across roads.

In other ways, in other places, the same scenario occurs wherever people settle undeveloped land. To mention only a few examples in the United States: Backhoes and dredging cranes alter the course of rivers and streams in a Louisiana backwater, disrupting the nests of snapping turtles; rangeland is expanded in the deserts of southeastern California, and the gopher tortoise suddenly must share its territory

Opposite page: A snapper confronts the handiwork of man—field fencing.

with cattle, sheep, and four-wheel-drive vehicles; the marshlands in the northeastern United States inhabited by the bog turtle continue to be drained and reclaimed.

ENVIRONMENTAL POLLUTION

Turtles undoubtedly suffer the short- and long-term effects of environmental pollution, especially in developed countries. As is the case with overdevelopment and disruption of their nesting sites, pollution is an "invisible" threat in that it is pervasive, low-profile (compared, say, to turtles being caught in shrimpers' nets), and to some degree simply taken for granted as a necessary accompaniment of population growth, movement, and industrialization.

The pollution of rivers, streams, and oceans with industrial by-products has driven untold thousands of aquatic turtles from their homes and nesting places and killed untold thousands more. Undoubtedly, many turtles and tortoises have been killed by the effects of herbicides and insecticides in the food they eat and the air they breathe. The poisons no doubt accumulate in the turtles' fat, though it is difficult at present to document the long-term and/or genetic effects of their exposure to pollutants and pesticides.

We know at least two examples of turtle species that are harmed by our careless treatment of the environment. Many giant leatherbacks die because they mistake plastic bags floating in the ocean for their favorite food, jellyfish, and in eating them fatally clog their digestive tracts.

Perhaps worse is the fate of the many hatchlings who seek out floating islands of seaweed, kelp, and sargassum in which to spend the first few years of their lives. Unfortunately, these sources of nourishment and camouflage also are places where oil, styrofoam, and tar collect. Baby turtles often die from ingesting these materials. Even if the hatchlings don't eat them, the oil and tar produce sores and lesions on the turtles' skins, which can lead to infection.

EFFORTS AT TURTLE CONSERVATION AND PROTECTION

The most successful attempts at conserving and protecting turtles—the only concerted efforts, actually—have occurred during the past forty years. (By "conservation," that is "regulating the use of," by establishing quotas on the numbers of turtles that can be killed, for example. "Protection," on the other hand, means "preventing an animal, or its eggs, from being destroyed.")

Measures of conservation and protection have taken basically two forms: government legislation and action by individuals and organized groups. An element essential to their success is the agreement and cooperation of the people most affected by the policies.

One obstacle to the effectiveness of modern conservation and protection efforts is that they are almost always complicated, requiring the cooperation of several interest groups or nations.

In general, conservation and protection measures are necessary only when the intentional or incidental killing of turtles reaches widespread proportions, which almost always takes place only when turtles are the victims of commercial processing.

Discussing threats to the green turtle in 1975, Archie Carr said, "More than anything, the commercialization of turtle meat and

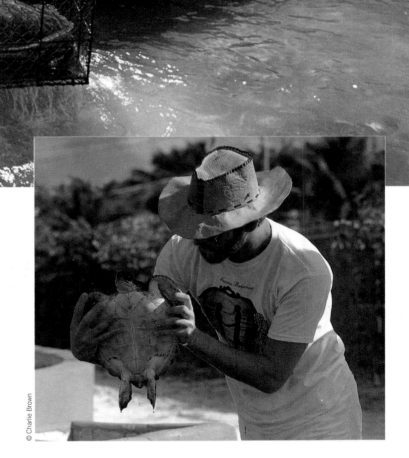

Upper left and upper right: Zoologists take a snapper's temperature and measurements, Great Swamp, New Jersey. *Above:* A turtle is transported from its breeding ground, while another is inspected *(right).*

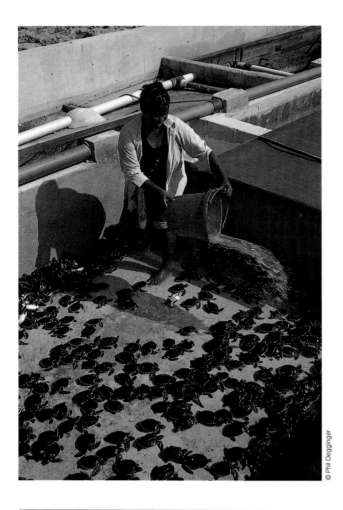

© Phil Degginger

Green turtle hatchlings in Grand Cayman.

LEGISLATION

products has pushed the species to the brink of extinction. It isn't the Indians eating a few turtles on the beach for subsistence. It isn't the coastal people sharing meat among themselves that's the problem, it's that mass marketing that's going on in world trade that is."

Why would someone resist measures of conservation and protection? Sometimes, people's livelihoods are at stake: those of the United States shrimpers, for instance. As Peter Pritchard says, "The desirability of conservation of a natural resource is obvious to anyone who is able to think beyond his immediate needs...[and] if it doesn't require any sacrifice. The desirability of protection is less widely recognized since its benefits are less concrete. In many cases, protection involves a definite inconvenience to people, or restriction of their activities, and may cost a lot of money."

Sometimes people's lives are at stake, and the choices that must be made are not easy. In his wonderful personal narrative, *Time of the Turtle,* Jack Rudloe recounts a trip to Haiti to find a live hawksbill for the Philadelphia Zoo. There, at the Baptist Mission near Port-au-Prince, he saw hawksbill shells and tortoiseshell items for sale and asked a missionary if she wasn't aware that, next to the Kemp's ridley, hawsbills were the most threatened of the sea turtles.

The missionary replied: "'I know that hawksbills are becoming extinct. But they're going to become extinct regardless of what we do. A big shell like that sells for two hundred dollars. Do you know how much *food* that can buy for these people?'"

Rudloe took a good look at the people of Haiti: "I looked about the streets outside the mission. I looked at the children with their bones almost protruding through their rib cages....Everywhere we went in Haiti, we were surrounded by a sea of beggars....The missionaries told us how in times of drought and famine parents would look over their children and decide which ones shouldn't be given any food and allowed to starve to death so the rest could live...

"I didn't have the answers. How do you preach conservation to people who are starving, and are struggling to survive on an hour-by-hour basis? Yet, if something isn't done, the hawksbill and every other creature will disappear, and these people will still starve in the end."

Nevertheless, choices have to be made, especially where large-scale commercial processing of turtles is concerned. Legislation has made possible protective options that were once inconceivable when the most powerful economic group in an area was simply allowed to do as it pleased with turtles.

On an international basis, for example, the Convention on International Trade in Endangered Species (CITES) created a treaty in 1979 prohibiting trade in turtle products made from endangered species. The United States signed the treaty, but unfortunately not all nations have.

Also, all seven species of marine turtles have been classed as Endangered or Vulnerable in the International Union for the Conservation of Nature (IUCN) *Red Data Book of Amphibians and Rep-*

tiles. This document has been instrumental in encouraging countries all over the world to compile lists of endangered species and pass laws to protect them.

In the United States, all marine turtles except the Australian flatback are listed with the United States Fish and Wildlife Service, and as such receive protection as Threatened or Endangered species under the Endangered Species Act (50 CFR 17.11). Several other species of turtles, such as the diamondback terrapin, are given federal protection.

Some individual states have undertaken projects involving sea turtles. For example, in the late 1970s, North Carolina began a sea turtle nesting surveillance program to determine the distribution and density of sea turtle nesting activity throughout the state; this was later supplemented by the North Carolina Sea Turtle Stranding Network and other programs.

In addition, most states have laws protecting tortoises from injury, harrassment, or even from being taken as pets. In a recent ruling (summer 1989), the U.S. Fish and Wildlife Service, alarmed by a sudden decline in the desert tortoise population, responded to an emergency request by environmental groups and gave protection to the California desert tortoise, the official state reptile, as an endangered species. In late 1989, off-road motorcycle races were prohibited in certain sections of the southern California desert because of the threat to the well-being of the desert tortoise.

Government action in behalf of turtles has been initiated in other countries, as well. In the 1970s, the governments of Surinam, South

Hope for future generations. Conservation for slow-moving creatures *(above)*; raising green turtles at Grand Cayman *(below)*.

EFFORTS OF INDIVIDUALS AND INDEPENDENT ORGANIZATIONS

America, and Queensland, Australia, made it illegal to kill turtles or dig up their eggs. In both cases, the governments were persuaded by the actions of one or two crusading individuals.

If a single person could be said to symbolize individuals and independent organizations committed to turtle conservation and protection, it would be the late Archie Carr, who died in 1987 at the age of 77.

Carr was interested in reptiles—particularly turtles—all his life. He became a professor of biology at the University of Florida in the late 1930s, and was an author, lecturer, researcher, and expert on the sea turtles, especially the green turtle.

In 1955, Carr became involved, in his words, "in a campaign to rehabilitate the green turtle in the Caribbean Sea," in part as a source of food for native peoples. He was able to get research grants from the National Science Foundation and the Office of Naval Research to study the migrations of the green turtle.

Carr began at Tortuguero Beach, Costa Rica, then the only remaining nesting beach for the green turtle in the western Caribbean, at first working to protect the nesting areas from egg poachers. In 1957, the government closed the beach to exploitation.

In conjunction with the Caribbean Conservation Corporation, which he helped found, Carr began a turtle-tagging program at Tortuguero Research Station in order to study turtle-migration patterns. In three decades, Carr and those who followed him tagged nearly 30,000 turtles.

In "Operation Green Turtle," Carr and his associates attempted to re-establish breeding colonies of green turtles in places they once had been. The CCC did this by taking thousands of eggs or hatchlings from Tortuguero to other sites, such as Florida, the Bahamas, and other locations in the Caribbean, for reintroduction to the ocean.

The late Archie Carr and a green turtle crawling back to the water after burying her eggs. Carr spent most of his life studying turtles and working to protect the green turtle.

Archie Carr's conservation efforts over a period of thirty years not only saved the green turtle in the western Caribbean from destruction, it inspired others—largely local people, government officials, and university students—to follow his example in other areas as well, such as at Escobilla Beach in Oaxaca, the principal nesting site of the olive ridley. There, Mexican university students volunteer to tag and count hatchlings emerging from the sand.

Basically, all successful attempts to conserve and protect turtles—whether at the governmental or independent level—will require the elements Archie Carr brought to the endeavor: intelligence, knowledge, passion, purpose, perspective, and the capacity to inspire others to share a vision of what might be and to act on that vision.

Other organizations promoting conservation and protection of turtles (and other animals) include the World Wildlife Fund, the Natural Resources Defense Council, the Environmental Defense Fund, the Defenders of Wildlife, and the New York Zoological Society.

A green turtle swimming gracefully in the South Pacific.

To conclude this section of the book, I want to relate two cautionary tales. The first is a Cheyenne legend concerning the origins of a pit in the High Plains region of Oklahoma.

Long ago, the story goes, forty-nine men from the same warrior society, armed with stone-bladed axes and spears, set out on foot with their chief to hunt buffalo. They walked for many days without seeing any game; finally, they decided to return to camp, crossing a barren area known as the Staked Plains.

The men saw something bright shining in the distance, but paid it little heed, thinking it was a mirage. As they came closer, the object increased in brightness, reflecting the light of the sun. All morning they moved toward the shining object, and when they got close enough they saw that it was a huge water turtle, traveling at a steady pace toward the next water hole.

For a while, the men walked beside the huge turtle. Then, impulsively, one man jumped on its back; others followed suit, until finally all stood on top of the turtle's carapace, save the chief. He urged the men to climb down, exclaiming that the turtle was a powerful and mysterious force not to be taken lightly.

Some of the men poked at the turtle's shell with their spears, but others thought better of it and tried to descend to the ground. It was then that the men discovered they were stuck fast to the turtle and could not get off. Full of fear, they attacked the turtle's head and limbs, but their weapons only broke into pieces.

The men shouted to their chief to save them. He tried to reason with the turtle, exclaiming that if the turtle released the warriors, the tribe would honor it forever. The turtle took no notice of the chief's pleadings; instead, it kept moving steadily onward. Late in the day, the chief saw the turtle's destination: a large, flat, dark body of water. The warriors saw it, too, and they began to pray and cry out to the turtle for mercy. But the turtle merely walked on.

At last, the chief cried to the men trapped on the turtle's back. "I have done all I can do," he said. "You discovered something wonderful, but you did not respect it. Now you will be punished because of the evil in your hearts."

Then the turtle entered the lake. The men on the turtle's back watched their chief at the water's edge and waved to him. Slowly they sank, as the turtle walked into deeper water. The water rose to their waists, to their chests, and finally flowed over their heads and waving arms. Then the turtle and the men disappeared entirely, and all was still. Shaken, the chief returned home alone to tell the terrible news to his people.

The second story comes from a chapter in Jack Rudloe's *Time of the Turtle,* describing an experience Rudloe had as a young man aboard a shrimp trawler that incidentally had caught a male and female loggerhead in its nets. Touched by their plight, Rudloe suggested to a deckhand that he let the turtles go. At the time, loggerheads could be sold at the dock, and the deckhand refused. Rudloe even offered to pay the going price. The deckhand, annoyed that the turtles had shredded his nets with their beaks, still refused.

Malagasy men closely watch the movements of a radiated tortoise. The bond between man and other creatures on the planet is tenuous, at best.

For a day, Rudloe watched the two turtles writhe helplessly on the ship's deck. When the ship docked, the time came to butcher the turtles. Rudloe silently watched the process—which he describes in grim and gory detail—filled with a mixture of fascination and repulsion.

"I really had mixed feelings about the shrimpers," he says. "They had been my friends, let me go out on their boats, and given me more practical experience in marine biology than I could have learned in five years spent in a classroom. Shrimpers were among the last . . . free men in our society. Yet by killing sea turtles, they were doing a bad thing. They were pushing an already overexploited species to the verge of extinction."

The crewman who had butchered the two turtles, noting Rudloe's despair, handed him a mass of eggs from inside the female. "'I know what you're thinking, Jack,' he said defensively. 'Well, I'll tell you this, and Preacher will back it up. There's millions of turtles out there, and this little bit that these boats catch don't amount to nothing. The fish eat their babies or the birds get 'em. You could kill a thousand turtles, ten thousand turtles, and it wouldn't hurt!'"

Previously, it has been stated that it may seem that we hold all the cards in our relations with turtles; the truth, however, is that turtles have a power over us which all subordinate beings hold: the power—based on our actions—to reveal who we really are, our regard for the planet, and (since we have the capacity to destroy the Earth) our prospects for survival.

The stories I have just recounted—one a legend, the other factual—illustrate this truth and provide the same lessons: The only way for an individual, a group, or the human race to live responsibly is to experience ourselves as a part of the planet and its creatures rather than as separate beings, and to act in awareness of a larger reality rather than focusing only on narrow, short-term needs.

The Cheyenne warriors, for instance, treated the giant turtle as something alien, learning too late that their fate and the turtle's were one and the same. Further, the warriors' deaths resulted from who they were and what they chose, and past a certain point their fate was inevitable—there was no going back, no chance to make different choices.

Similarly, the turtle butcher created a narrow picture of reality based on his own needs rather than the facts ("You could kill . . . ten thousand turtles, and it wouldn't hurt!"). Had he been able to see beyond himself and acknowledge the precariousness of the loggerhead's existence, he might have released the animals instead of killing them.

Both stories presuppose an unstated condition: To learn anything of value from what turtles are trying to tell to us, we must first be listening. Are we? Some people, the Archie Carrs of the world, are. Others, the shrimpers who refuse to use TEDs, for instance, still have a distorted view of nature and the place of human beings in it.

That view, molded by greed and fear, could be summarized as follows: "Nature is there to be used as we see fit. Turtles stand between us and the shrimp. If we don't get the shrimp (each crew says), someone else will. Turtles are a nuisance, an inconvenience—they have to be sacrificed. Too bad, but that's the way it is." How else is it possible to explain the views of Southern congressmen who, speaking in behalf of the shrimpers, said that protecting a nearly extinct species is "shortsighted" and that relaxing the rules requiring the use of TEDs was "morally the right thing to do"?

Any fragile, integrated system can only stand so much abuse before it breaks down—in small, imperceptible ways or large, catastrophic ones. When turtles disappear in large numbers—through excessive killing, environmental poisoning, or simple neglect—it should serve as a warning that our lives and that of the planet are somehow out of balance, in ways that may be difficult or impossible to remedy.

In pre-industrial times, many Native Americans who lived by hunting and subsistence farming took the view that animals are too intelligent and powerful to fall prey to a hunter, but that animals understand that people need to eat, and so they sacrifice themselves from a sense of compassion. But for this arrangement to continue, human beings must have respect for animals and take only what they need; greed will be punished by the spirits.

In my view, we will have to begin to experience life in this way if we are to save the lives of turtles, other endangered species, and the planet. We will have to relinquish a certain power and arrogance that is deeply ingrained in industrial society.

Given that the lives of all creatures on the planet are inevitably and inextricably tied to one another, what will it take to survive? Resolute people who will put kindness and humanity in place of material progress. The absence of greed. Respect for nature and truth.

It is uncertain if such a transformation can take place, but we must act as if it can. We must make the viewpoint expressed in an old Pennsylvania Dutch proverb our own: We do not inherit the Earth from our ancestors; we borrow it from our children. Otherwise, in Archie Carr's words: "What we keep of the old earth will not be enough to save our honor with our descendants."

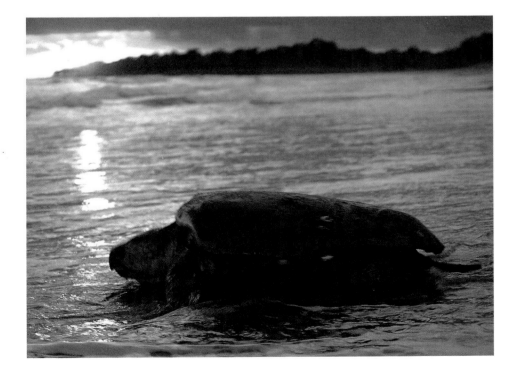

What will be its fate? A loggerhead reenters the surf after depositing her eggs.

B I B L I O G R A P H Y

Alderton, David. *Turtles and Tortoises of the World.* New York: Facts on File, 1988.

Bjorndal, Karen A. (ed.) *Biology and Conservation of Sea Turtles.* Washington, D.C.: Smithsonian Institution Press, 1982.

Bustard, H. Robert. *Sea Turtles: Their Natural History and Conservation.* New York: Taplinger Publishing Co., 1972.

Carr, Archie. *Handbook of Turtles: The Turtles of the United States, Canada and Baja California.* Ithaca, NY: Comstock Publishing Assoc., a division of Cornell University Press, 1952.

___*The Reptiles.* Alexandria, VA: Time-Life Books, 1977.

___*So Excellent a Fish: A Natural History of Sea Turtles.* Garden City, NY: Doubleday & Co., 1973, rev. 1977.

Cobb, Jo. *A Complete Introduction to Turtles and Terrapins.* Neptune City, NJ: T.F.H. Publications, 1987.

Ernst, Carl H., and Barbour, Roger W. *Turtles of the United States.* Lexington, KY: University Press, 1972.

Gibbons, Whit. *Their Blood Runs Cold: Adventures With Reptiles and Amphibians.* University, AL: The University of Alabama Press, 1977.

Holling, Holling Clancy. *Minn of the Misssssippi.* Boston: Houghton Mifflin, 1951.

Jocher, Willy. *Turtles for Home and Garden.* Neptune City, NJ: T.F.H. Publications, 1973.

Nicholls, Richard E. *The Running Press Book of Turtles.* Philadelphia: Running Press, 1977.

Obst, Fritz J. *Turtles, Tortoises and Terrapins.* New York: St. Martin's Press, 1986.

Pope, Clifford. *Turtles of the United States and Canada.* New York: Alfred Knopf, 1939.

Pritchard, Peter C.H. *Encyclopedia of Turtles.* Neptune City, NJ: T.F.H. Publications, 1979.

Reidman, Sarah R. and William, Ross. *Turtles: Extinction or Survival?* New York: Abelard-Schuman, 1974.

Rudloe, Jack. *Time of the Turtle.* New York: Alfred A. Knopf, Inc., 1979.

Smith, Hobart M., and Brodie, Edmund D. Jr. *Reptiles of North America: A Guide to Field Identification.* New York: Golden Press, 1982.

Zappalorti, Robert T. *The Amateur Zoologists Guide to Turtles and Crocodilians.* Harrisburg, PA: Stackpole Books, 1976.

Turtle and Wildlife Organizations

California Turtle and Tortoise Club
P.O. Box 90252
Los Angeles, CA 90009

Caribbean Conservation Corp.
P.O. Box 2866
Gainesville, FL 32602

Center for Marine Conservation
1725 DeSales St., N.W.
Washington, D.C. 20036

Desert Tortoise Preserve Committee, Inc.
P.O. Box 453
Ridgecrest, CA 94133

Earth Island Institute
300 Broadway
San Francisco, CA 94133

Freshwater Turtles and Land Tortoise Specialists Group
(affiliated with the International Union for the Conservation of Nature—IUCN):

Michael Klemens, director of global program
Department of Herpetology and Icthyology
American Museum of Natural History
Central Park West at 79th St.
New York, N.Y. 10024

Durrel Institute of Conservation and Ecology
University of Kent
Canterbury, Kent, United Kingdom CT27NY

Florida Audubon Society
1101 Audubon Way
Maitland, FL 32751

Greenpeace International
1436 U St., N.W.
Washington, D.C. 20009

HEART (Ridley Turtles)
P.O. Box 681231
Houston, TX 77268-1231

National Wildlife Federation
1400 16th St., N.W.
Washington, D.C. 20036-2266

New York Turtle and Tortoise Society
365 Pacific Street
Brooklyn, NY 11217

Sea Turtle Center
P.O. Box 634
Nevada City, CA 95959

World Wildlife Fund and The Conservation Foundation
1250 24th St., N.W.
Washington, D.C. 20037

INDEX

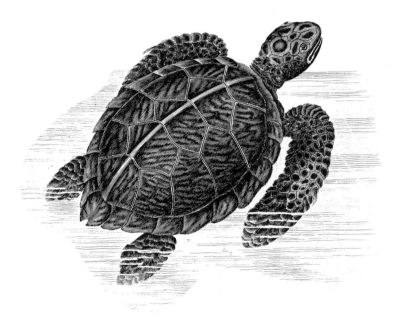